The Eyes of the Heart

The Biblical Path to Spirituality and Inner

Empowerment

By

Albert C. Gaw, M.D.

xulon
PRESS

The Eyes of the Heart
The Biblical Path to Spirituality and Inner Empowerment
by Albert C. Gaw, M.D.

Printed in the United States of America

ISBN 978-1-60266-979-6

www.xulonpress.com

3/17/09

Dear Tien Li,

With best wishes,

Uncle Albert

I pray also that the ***eyes of your heart*** may be enlightened in order that you may know the hope to which he has called you, the riches of his glorious inheritance in the saints, and his incomparably great power for us who believe.

Paul's letter to the *Ephesians* (1:18-19)

In loving memory of my mother, Chao Huang Huang and the late Rev. Henry Michael and Stella Elda Veenschoten, Reformed Church missionaries to China and the Philippines whose lives touched many, including mine.

About the author:

Albert C. Gaw, MD, is a board-certified psychiatrist and a Distinguished Life Fellow of the American Psychiatric Association. A practicing psychiatrist for more than forty years. Dr. Gaw is currently a Clinical Professor of Psychiatry at the University of California Medical School at San Francisco and the Medical Director of Quality Management for San Francisco's Community Behavioral Health Services.

Dr. Gaw was a Professor of Cross-Cultural Psychiatry at the University of Massachusetts Medical School at Worcester, Massachusetts; a Clinical Professor of Psychiatry at Boston University School of Medicine; and a Lecturer on Psychiatry at Harvard Medical School.

Dr. Gaw's abiding interest in providing holistic care to persons in distress has taken him to explore the integration of biology, psychology, anthropology, sociology, and theology. This book can be seen as the author's attempt to explore the interface between Christian spirituality and psychology and as a step toward the integration of spirituality in wellness and healing in the Christian context.

Dr. Gaw is the recipient of the Filipinas Magazine's Achievement Award in Medicine in 2002, the Meritorious Service Award of the Northern California Psychiatric Society in 2004, and the Kun-Po Soo Asian American Award of the American Psychiatric Association in 2006.

Among many of his writings and publications are three books: **Cross-Cultural Psychiatry**, published by Wright PSG Press; **Culture, Ethnicity and Mental Illness**; and **Concise Guide to Cross-Cultural Psychiatry**, both published by the American Psychiatric Press, Inc. Dr. Gaw is the author of the chapter "Cultural Issues," **Textbook of Clinical Psychiatry**, 5th Edition (Washington, DC: American Psychiatric Publishing, Inc., 2008).

Contents

Preface

Why would a psychiatrist write a book on spirituality? I believe many psychiatrists and a great number of the public have neglected spirituality which is an important area — in living and in healing. Many psychiatrists have regarded the matters of the "soul" as phenomena projected upon it by the unconscious mind and dismiss its significance in their patient's life. The mentality of the public that believes in instant nirvana and gratification that pervades our modern world have blinded us from a spiritual truth—that humans are spiritual beings, capable of supreme love, of art and of beauty. The scientific revolutions that have created miracles such as cloning and other genetic breakthroughs have caused some to think that we could build our modern Tower of Babel, that we could reach heaven by means of human inventions. The media has conditioned us to want superficial ideas and material things and their use of subliminal messages has numbed us to shun matters of the soul and the interiority of our beings. By short-changing spirituality, I believe we have ignored a vast reserve of creative spiritual energy. We are stuck at a level of existence that feeds us nothing but meaninglessness and helplessness. I feel if we want to acquire the power of the spiritual energy in order to meet the challenges we all face, to find meanings in life, and to enhance our health and happiness, then we cannot ignore our spirituality.

But what is spirituality? How does one explore its depths? And how could one achieve a higher degree of spirituality? These challenges prompted me to turn to the bible and to take a fresh look at spirituality from a biblical perspective. The bible contains rich deposits of human experience that provide profound insights into what makes up our spiritual core. It offers useful guidelines for living, including guidelines to us in our relationship to others, in our relation to the physical world, and to God. Although it is not a therapeutic book, biblical messages can have significant implications for our physical, emotional and spiritual health. Biblical spiritual messages can become even more alive when their psychological dimension is understood and applied to daily life and work, not in a blind and judgmental manner, but in a spirit of truth, tolerance, and magnanimity.

Since I am a product of the Christian tradition and have always been interested in the bible, I decided to use the biblical teaching about spirituality as a paradigm of study and explore how its concepts apply both to practical living and as a tool for health and well-being. And I wanted to examine biblical concepts of spirituality through the lens of a psychiatrist, a clinician, a lay Christian, and one interested in holistic healing while not deviating from their original textual messages. Toward this end and within the pages of this book, I bring my understanding of the workings of the mind as a medical doctor and a psychiatrist and my psychological insights into human-in-distress into the discourse on spirituality in the following ways:

1) I used current medical knowledge of "stress" and how the human mind copes with it to analyze the life stresses faced by biblical characters and to show how their psychological make-up influenced their spirituality and vice-versa.

2) I applied modern psychological constructs such as personality theory, character, self-esteem, narcissism; neurobiological correlation of cognition, emotion, feeling and behavior; psychiatric concepts of unconscious mental life, unconscious mental defense mechanisms; the mental status examination; concepts of psychological and psychiatric disorders; principles of psychiatric treatment and healing in order to explicate the hidden intra-psychic experiences of biblical characters

such as King Saul, King David and the prophet Jonah in the Old Testament and to shed light on key events in their lives.

3) I used modern psychological precepts and language to explain biblical concepts of Christian spirituality and examined what could be the psychological processes in the transformation of the mind and the changes that could be brought about in one's personality in the area of thinking, feeling, behavior and interpersonal relationship when one acted on faith to believe in Christ and followed his teachings.

4) I drew on my neurobiological understanding of the integrated human mind in thinking, emotion, feeling and behavior in order to advance the idea that an authentic Christian spiritual life involved a transformation in the totality of the personality and in the alignment of these components of the mind with the teaching of Christ and not just with the intellect alone.

5) I tried to show how an appreciation of the socio-political-religious and cultural background of the time molded and shaped the responses of certain biblical characters in the Old Testament and influenced the thinking and writing of key New Testament writers and how this approach to the study the bible could enrich biblical understanding.

Thus, this book is a series of my reflections on biblical spirituality. It represents my attempt to integrate biblical teachings in both my own spiritual journey and in my psychiatric practice. It is intended for persons interested in gaining insight into spirituality from an Evangelical Christian perspective. It can be used as a reference guide for teaching in churches and Sunday Schools. And it includes exhortations that readers may find useful. For professionals in the mental health field, this book can be seen as my attempt to explore the inter-phase between spirituality and psychology within one faith tradition. I hope the paradigm I used here will encourage others to seek and study the integration of spirituality and psychology in other faith traditions as well.

Since I recognize that there is a current debate over the authorship of various books in the bible that I am quoting from, I want to state at the onset my thinking over the authorship of the bible. I have been taught that all scriptures were the inspired words of God. (2 Timothy 3:16) I hold the position that the authorship of the various letters in the New Testament indeed were ascribed to the authors mentioned in the epistles even though I recognize that there are other views. Thus, I assumed that the letters to the Romans, Galatians, First and Second Corinthians, Galatians, Ephesians, Philippians, Colossians, First and Second Thessalonians, First and Second Timothy, Titus, Philemon and Hebrews were ascribed to Paul; the letter of James to James, the brother of Christ; the First and Second Epistles of Peter to Peter, Christ's disciple; and the Gospel of John to John, another Christ's disciple. In so doing, I am also relying on the authority of their written words and in the process of analyzing the biblical passages, I may have conveyed their messages in an emotional "tone" that is much more "authoritative" than what I would have intended, as reflected in the first and third section of this book.

In reading Paul's prayer to the Ephesians, I was awestruck by his use of the metaphor of the "eyes of the heart" as a way to gain hope, knowledge, and power for those who believe. (Ephesians 1:18-19) Here was a man of profound spiritual insight who was trying to tell us that we must seek spirituality through *the eyes of the heart*. I determined to take Paul's advice seriously and using his metaphor of the *eyes of the heart* launched a psycho-spiritual study of the teachings of three key figures in the New Testament and then looked at the lives of three selected men in the Old Testament. From these studies, I selected six common psychological themes that organize the biblical messages. Each theme reflects an important aspect of one's personality make-up, i.e. in the area of cognition, behavior, and emotion and represents clinical issues I frequently encountered in my practice. I have also added a contemporary psychological perspective to the understanding of the "mind" of the biblical characters in order to provide a "bridge" that connects the deep emotional matters of the "soul" to outer behavioral manifestations. By bringing together spiritual revelations and contemporary psychological perspectives, I hope to provide an enriched, balanced, and integrated perspective to an understanding of spirituality and the lessons of the bible, and thus, avoid the trap of either explaining all human behavior only through the lens of the bible (pan-theologizing) or explaining every biblical idea or tenet of belief through the eyes of psychology (pan-psychologizing).[1]

The book's organization reflects these thoughts. The first section, "Transforming Words," serves as the theoretical basis of Christian spirituality. It consists of the themes selected from the writings of Paul, Peter and James in the New Testament. The *eyes of the heart* of these three men are examined to unlock the secret of their spirituality. Although their writings do not cover the entire treatise of Christian theology, taken together, I believe they provide a sufficiently harmonious and robust body of theoretical concepts about the Christian mind. This conceptual understanding can help us with the process of achieving Christian spirituality. The second section, "Challenges of Spirituality," analyzes the lives of King Saul, King David and the prophet Jonah in the Old Testament from a psycho-spiritual perspective. It attempts to explain how each of these men's spirituality and the interplay with their psychological issues facilitated their success in life or hastened their failure. "Path to Spirituality," the third section, sums up how the Christ's teachings can help us achieve this important human spiritual dimension. At the end of each chapter, I have listed the key points from the chapter.

Thus, the themes and content of each chapter can be listed this way:

1. What is spirituality? William James's working definition of religion is used to explore the psychological and cultural dimension of spirituality. I explicate the use of the concept of "mind in culture" as an analytic tool to probe spirituality.
2. Power Life: The Book of Ephesians. Paul's metaphor of the "eyes of the heart" is explained to unlock the secret of Christian spirituality. Using the analogy of the field of electric power dynamics, I analyze Paul's concept of a powerful spiritual life.
3. Wholesome Thinking: First and Second Peter. Peter's use of the concept of "wholesome thinking" is analyzed to show how the changes in the thought processes and in the stages of spiritual growth and development lead to a fuller Christian spiritual life.

4. Authentic Life: Book of James. James's messages on the integration of faith and works and his emphasis on the behavioral manifestations of Christian spirituality are used in order to show how to achieve an authentic Christian spiritual life.

5. Self-esteem: Life of King Saul. King Saul's lack of spirituality and how that affected his self-esteem are looked at in order to understand his downward emotional spiral resulting in his suicide.

6. Character Flaws: Life of Jonah. Jonah's character flaws are analyzed to show how his emotional and spiritual "blind spots" created the paradox of this prophet's plea for death at the height of his success.

7. Integrity: Life of King David. Six episodes from King David's life are analyzed to portray the effects of how his spirituality and integrity led to his spiritual redemption despite his flaws and blunders.

8. Christ on Spirituality. Christ's teachings on spirituality sum up the Master's path to achieving spirituality that can lead to the attainment of a rich, fulfilling, and powerful life.

Since the apostles share a certain commonality of thinking, it is inevitable that there are overlaps in and repetitions of their spiritual concepts and teachings. For example, both Paul and Peter in their respective chapter teach what the new relationship between wives and husbands *in Christ* means. Where these occurred, I have retained their precepts in the chapter and crossed-referenced them, so that each chapter can be read alone.

Within these pages, I tried to illustrate the relevance of the biblical messages to our spiritual lives and how to apply them to our daily living. My hope is that we will all discover the power of beliefs and how to use it to help us tap into our spiritual reservoir in order to meet the challenges we all face today.

Albert C. Gaw, M.D.
San Francisco

Disclaimers:

The opinions expressed in this book are strictly my own and do not reflect official statements, positions, or policies of the Department of Psychiatry, the University of California at San Francisco; the Department of Public Health of the City and County of San Francisco; or those of the American Psychiatric Association.

Acknowledgments

The seed and genesis of this book owes much to many individuals who have influenced and shaped my life and spiritual journey.

- The late Reverent Silas Wong first introduced me to Christ when I was a junior student at Hope Christian High School in Manila, Philippines.
- The late Miss Tena Holkeboer and the late Reverend Joseph and Marion Esther, Reformed Church of America missionaries to the Philippines, were my spiritual mentors and teachers.
- Miss Encarnacion Go Beltran and the late Gregoria Go Beltran were inspiring teachers at Hope Christian High School in Manila, Philippines.
- The late Rev. and Mrs. Henry Michael Veenschoteen encouraged and supported me through medical school.
- Jack Hill, M.D., psychiatrist encouraged me to go into psychiatry.
- The late Dr. Jaime Zaguirre at the University of the East, Ramon Magsaysay Memorial Medical Center in Quezon City, the Philippines taught me the model of the integrated human person.
- The late Drs. John Romano, George Engel, and Otto Thaler of the Department of Psychiatry at the University of Rochester Medical School, Rochester, New York, were influential

in molding my thinking about integrated biopsychosocial approaches to the human person.

- Arthur Kleinman, M.D. of the Department of Anthropology and Psychiatry at Harvard University introduced me to the exciting field of cultural psychiatry and the concept of "socio-somatic medicine."

Bridging the gap between spirituality and psychology is a daunting challenge. I am indebted to both biblical scholar and psychiatric colleagues for their useful comments and feedback. My colleagues Sara Charles, M.D. and Jack Hill, M.D. provided useful critique. The Rev. Dr. James G. Emerson, Jr., past President of San Francisco Theological Seminary and continuing Adjunct Professor reviewed my discussion of biblical spirituality from the Evangelical theological perspective and helped me clarified some of the scriptural passages. Deborah Emin, editor, provided excellent editorial assistance. Tina, my wife, as always, has been the silent partner throughout the preparation of this volume. But above all, the primary source for the inspiration of this volume has been Christ—my way, my truth and my life.

My prayer is that you too will find joy in the discovery of biblical truths through these psychological explanations and obtain emotional strength through the spiritual insights they afford.

Albert C. Gaw, M.D.
San Francisco

1. What is Spirituality?

Spirituality is subjective. Its authenticity is embedded in human experience. Like a person in love, spirituality cannot hide. Its manifestations are palpable. Its essence is present in all aspects of living.

Some writers tried to differentiate spirituality from religion. Religion is sometimes referred to as the external, ritualistic practice of one's religious faith. Often it refers to "a particular tradition, practice, or community that shapes a comprehensive world-view sufficient to interpret all of human experience within a specific cultural context."[1] William James considered the external, institutional aspects of religion as "an external art, the art of winning the favors of the gods."[2] On the other hand, spirituality refers to the inner core of one's religious beliefs and is attributed to "the nearly universal human search for meaning, often involving some sense of transcendence."[3] It refers to "any religious or ethical value that is concretized as an attitude or spirit from which one's action flows."[4] It is akin to what James referred to as "the more personal branch of religion...the inner dispositions of man himself which forms the centre of interest, his conscience, his deserts, his helplessness, his incompleteness."[5] Both spirituality and religion can be used to define the meaning of our existence. Like yin/yang, spirituality and religion really cannot be separated as Descartes did with the mind and body. They must be viewed in a totality.[6] Although the emphasis may be different, they refer to the same phenomenon.

Let us look closer at how William James describes religion. Dr. William James, a Harvard physician and philosopher was considered the most famous American psychologist at the turn of the 20th century. In his famous Gifford Lectures on the *Varieties of Religious Experiences*, which he gave in Scotland in 1902, he proposed this working definition of religion: "*Religion*, therefore, as I now ask you to arbitrarily to take it, shall mean for us the *feelings, acts, and experiences of individual men in their solitude, so far as they apprehend themselves to stand in relation to whatever they may consider the divine*."[7] Although James felt that relation may be "moral, physical or ritual", it was the immediate personal experience that he wanted to emphasize. He tried to address the psychological processes that may occur when we encountered aspects of our experience that we considered "divine."

But what is "divine'? James used this term "divine" broadly to mean "any object that is god*like*, whether it be a concrete deity or not."[8] James tried to provide a generic definition. He argued that there are systems of thoughts that could stir in us strong sentiments called *religious sentiments* that are as real as any concretized experience that our sensory organs could evoke. Buddhists, Christians, artists and philosophers and all of us could share this religious sentiment that James described as "divine."

James went on to define the qualities of being god*like*. "Gods are conceived to be first things in ways of being and power."[9] Something is "godlike" when we relate to them as the first and the last word in the way of truth. "They overarch and envelop, and from them there is no escape."[10] To James, religion is man's *total reaction upon life.*[11] It encompasses not just the content of one's beliefs, but also involves the one's total attitude toward existence as well. James asserted that a man's total reaction is different from the casual ones just as total attitudes are different from casual or professional attitudes. He felt that in order to get at these total reactions, we have to go beyond the attitude of looking at mere existence and to reach deeply within oneself to get a sense of that meaning of life that he described as "that curious sense of the whole residual cosmos as an everlasting presence."[12] What encapsulates our individual sense of the universe in which we dwell and how we express it were regarded by James as religious reactions. The divine connotes a primal reality that the individual feels compelled to respond to solemnly and gravely. It is always serious. It contains elements or qualities of experiences that we can meet nowhere else.[13] True religion can hold our center when all else in life around us crumbles or is stripped away. It allows an individual to sing while being imprisoned for no offense other than the desire to practice or hold unto one's beliefs. It differs from morality in the manner with which we accept the universe. James argued that morality accepts the law of the universe in part or grudgingly. But the religious attitude accepts it whole-heartedly and altogether. We submit to the divine with a cheerful or glad attitude. And in this sense, religion exceeds the moral frame of mind.[14] No wonder religious sentiment can motivate a person to travel to the deepest African jungle in order to build a hospital or a church, or to scale the highest mountain peak in order to plant a flag or set up a shrine for worship. Conversely, if religious sentiment is applied in a distorted way, we witness phenomenon in which one is willing to commit acts of violence as in blowing oneself up in the name of religion, or to systematically wipe out another race of people in the name of enhancing genetic purity. Religious sentiments could evoke such a total reaction to life. And that sentiment must be applied to life situations intelligently, judiciously and with love. Whether it becomes a positive or negative influence depends on the context in which religious sentiment is applied.

Because James's definition of religion and his usage of the "more personal branch of religion" come closest to the areas of psychological issues I want to explore, for the purposes of this book, we shall adopt James's definition of *personal religion* to mean spirituality.

If we can paraphrase James's descriptions of a spiritual life and apply it to the definition of Christian spirituality, it would consist of the following: when in one's solitude, a person professes a belief in an Almighty God that shapes his total reaction to life; who finds elements of experiences that can meet nowhere else; who willingly holds the teaching of Christ and the bible as the highest ideals and authority for one's actions; who feels compelled to act solemnly and gravely in fulfilling Christ's and the bible's commandments; who can experience joy in the midst of human suffering; and is willing to *perform* service of the highest without complaint, that person feels the subjective *feelings* that partially defines the "divine" of Christian spirituality.

But how can we determine the authenticity of religious sentiments? This is revealed through the *action* that flows from such sentiment. James emphasized what Christ mentioned in Matthew 7:16 that the authenticity of religion is borne out by the "fruits" of the actions of an individual. The transformation of a religious sentiment into an action may be as dramatic as that of Paul's experience on the road to Damascus. Or it can be gradual, as in Peter's experience in coming to grips with the person of Christ. And when their actions are viewed as Paul or Peter's total reaction to life after their encounter with Christ, we can get a glimpse of their spirituality.

As I am using spirituality here, it suggests a quieter, more gradual, almost imperceptible transformation of the totality of the personality of an individual that is sustained over time. The change affects all realms of the personality: cognition, emotion, and behavior. It is an on-going process. That change is linked to the idea of a higher order, as in a belief in God. Personal events such as a survival from a catastrophic car accident or gaining balance after a loss, could initiate this change. As a result, there is a gradual expression of a religious sentiment that defines more sharply the contour of the purpose of one's existence. It provides an individual with a sense of persistent inner peace and a confidence to move through life with a realization of living in a state of grace. To such individuals, daily events and their perception of them assume a different significance. The rose seems to smell sweeter, the day seems brighter, and there seem to be ubiquitous opportunities to do good deeds (as in the satisfaction that comes from the simple act of picking up a banana peel to prevent others from slipping and falling as one strolls down the street). Although one can move through one's daily life without being visibly noticed by others, a process of transformation of character continues to evolve until one finds bliss in coming to terms with one's purpose of existence and in unity with one's ego-ideal as reflected in an identification with the perceived character of one's Creator.

Christian spirituality, then, is centered on the belief of the Judeo-Christian God, "as revealed in Jesus Christ, and experienced through the gifts of the Holy Spirit." [15]

Before I embark on a discussion about the spirituality of specific persons in the bible, let me first explain the method I used in the study of the bible. I employed the psycho-spiritual approach that concerns exploring the *mind in the context of culture.* [16] Mind, spirituality and culture are inter-related. The mind is the result of the operation of the brain and is the connection between the individual and his or her material and non-material environment. The "mind' of an individual is revealed through patterns of thoughts, feelings and behavior that are fairly consistent over time and these form the distinctive features of one's personality. Culture, on the other hand, is that "complex whole which includes knowledge, belief, art, law, morals, custom and any other capabilities and habits acquired by man as a member of society," [17] It is that collective whole that serves as the context that defines the significance of one's act and that gives meaning to one's words and behavior. Cultural patterns are transmitted through symbols as in words and artifacts. When these symbols are embodied in external artifacts such as the pyramids of Egypt, they are what anthropologist Goodenough called the *objective order of reality.*[18] But there is another aspect to cultural patterns that is subjective. It includes traditional ideas and their attached values, beliefs, and operating procedures [19] these operate in a person's mind and constitute the individual's subjective culture (*subjective order of reality*). This subjective culture is as "real" to the individual as the objective culture just as the fragrance of a rose is to a rose petal. Because the human mind constantly interacts with its environment, the mind and its cultural environment cannot be separated. The psycho-spiritual approach analyses the operation of the mind and takes into consideration the social, political and religious background that give meanings to a person's ideas and behavior. Viewed in this way, spirituality is part of the *subjective order of reality* of an individual. It deals with how the conscious and unconscious mind impact on an individual's spirituality. Conversely, the social, political, religious and historical times in which a person lives also affect how one thinks, feels and acts and these could also influence one's spirituality. I want to employ the analysis of this subjective culture of the human mind as a tool to explore the domain of experience that James defined as *religion*.

Thus, we can look at the psycho-spiritual concept as an analytical tool in order to understand the spirituality of biblical characters. The experience of Saul of Tarsus is a dramatic and vivid example. An educated Jew, a Pharisee, an intellectual who zealously guarded his religious traditions and beliefs, Saul was on the road to Damascus to persecute the early Christians when he had a conversion experience and became a Christian. He went on to become the major intellectual pillar of Christianity. A tireless missionary, he was responsible for spreading the gospel of Christ to many parts of the world. The transformation of his character and identity was total. He described his experiences in numerous letters to the early churches—the epistle to the Romans, Galatians, Philippians, Galatians, Colossians, etc. By analyzing his thoughts, actions and experiences, we can understand the changes in his thinking, emotions and behavior caused by this experience on his way to Damascus. In a way, he experienced a profound cultural change in his mind and personality structure as reflected in changes in his percepts, concepts, propositions, beliefs, values, and ways of doing things. By analyzing the changes of these subjective cultural parameters of St. Paul, we can obtain an even deeper understanding of his mind and appreciate his spirituality.

Having provided these definitions of spirituality and culture and with the explication of the method of my study, I now invite you to explore the spiritual mind of selected prominent individuals in the Bible with me so that you can see how you can apply these same ideas about spirituality and culture in your reading of the bible and in your lives too.

KEY POINTS:

- Spirituality is a subjective experience that can be studied and understood.

- William James's working definition of "personal religion" is a paradigm to understand the psychology of spirituality.

- Christian spirituality is centered on the belief of the Judeo-Christian God as revealed in Jesus Christ, and experienced through the gifts of the Holy Spirit.

- The psycho-spiritual approach is used as a conceptual tool to study spirituality.

- Culture serves within a context that imbues human behavior, with meaning.

- Culture consists of both the objective and subjective orders of reality.

- The mind forms a connection between one's material and non-material worlds.

SECTION 1:

THE TRANSFORMING WORDS

2. Paul: Power Life

SIGNIFICANCE:

Acquire spiritual power. It will give you new sources of energy to meet life's challenges.

Paul

**"I pray ... that the *eyes of your heart* may be enlight-
ened in order that you may know... his incomparable
great *power* for us who believe." (Ephesians 1:18-19)**

Introduction

W hy did Paul use the metaphor of the "eyes of the heart" to
unravel spiritual power?[1] Spiritual power, as Paul implied it,
is not primarily a left-brain activity, the result of so-called "scientific
deductions" alone. The logical "eyes" of the mind cannot understand matters of the spirit. Spirituality must be seen and understood
with the "eyes of the heart."

Paul wanted the Ephesians to understand this. He started his
prayer by asking God to give them the spirit of wisdom and revelation. Then he also prayed for the enlightenment of the "eyes of
their hearts" so that they may know the hope of the riches of God's
glorious inheritance in the saints, and to obtain incomparable great
power for them who believe. To Paul, spiritual wisdom was revealed,
based on faith.

In his letter to the Hebrews, the author defined faith as "being sure
of what we hope for and certain of what we do not *see*." (Hebrews
11:1) It is through the "eyes of the heart" that one can begin to come
to an understanding of matters pertaining to the spirit. To have faith
does not mean the suspension of one's reasoning power; rather, one

must be willing to consider the reality of another realm of human experience, the domain of the "spirit." This is the great stumbling block for men of science who are trained to believe based on the evidence of "objective facts." To accept certain tenets and experiences as a matter of faith is viewing things beyond the physical eye which is not the way men of science are trained to do. To discern spirituality, as Paul implied, one has to be willing and able to see these things through the "eyes of the heart."

To illustrate Paul's assertion, we will examine the insight Paul has through the *eyes of his heart* into the relationship of his concept of God, the glorious father, to the obtainment of spiritual power in Christ as he described it in his letter to the Ephesians.

Power Life

Power life can be viewed from a field of energy perspective. A powerful spiritual life comes across as vibrant and energetic much like a computer powered by a full battery or a car running on a full-tank of gasoline. On the other hand, the lack of energy can create a gloomy picture and is reflected in a sense of helplessness. If we use the energy crisis in California in the year 2001 as an apt description of the emotional state of human affairs today, we can make some parallels between New Testament time and today. In 2001, electricity had to be rationed which meant lights in buildings had to be either dimmed or shut off. People worried about whether there would be enough electrical energy to run the essential services that sustained their daily lives. I see this kind of helplessness in my daily work as a psychiatrist, where I am constantly confronted by individuals feeling helpless to change their state of depression, addictive problems, thought disorders, mood problems or their challenges in fostering better relationships. To many, life feels like that energy crisis when all of the power they needed to keep going must be shut off or they might run out of energy. It makes them feel as if their life is like a motor boat running out of gasoline and sputtering to a stop in a vast ocean. It can be quite scary!

Reading Paul's letter to the believers in Ephesus, a word stands out—power! He wrote about "the incomparable great *power* for us who believe." (Ephesians 1:19) In his prayer for the Ephesians, he asked for the strengthening of the inner being of the believers with *power* through the Holy Spirit. (Ephesians 3:16) He wanted the Ephesians to acquire spiritual power and he laid out how one could obtain it.

Could Paul have been pointing to a vast untapped reserve of creative energy resources that modern man frequently neglects or ignores? And if so, how can one tap into that vast energy field?

Since power can best be understood in terms of field of energy dynamics and there is clinical relevance referring to various energy states (e.g., depressed patients have low energy level and manic patients have high energy level) and treatment procedure such as Transcranial Magnetic Stimulation (TMS)[2] that aims to alter brain's energy level, I chose to examine Paul's entire letter to the Ephesians and organizing its meanings of *power* from an energy field perspective. If we draw the analogy between electrical energy and spiritual energy, we can consider several aspects of power needs and generation: First, the architect must create a total power plan. Then generators convert water energy into electricity. The electricity is stored in power plants. From the power plants, cables are used to bring electricity to each individual household user. We use switches to turn on lights and run electrical appliances. Inside the cables or electrical wiring is electricity, something our naked eyes cannot see, but we can feel it when we touch a live wire. And when electricity is used to turn on the bulbs of a chandelier, we notice how beautiful a chandelier can be. Thus, applying the analogy of the field of electrical energy dynamics to spirituality, one can use this analogy to think about spiritual energy and power and the following questions can be asked:

1. What is God's power plan?
2. Where is the source or reservoir of spiritual power?
3. How can we get connected to God's power source?
4. What is God's power generator?
5. What is the "switch" that can turn on spiritual power?
6. What is the powerful spiritual current?
7. What are the effects or manifestations of a powerful spiritual life?

Ephesians

God's power plan

Paul asserted that God has a power plan. God's power plan lies in the obtainment of spiritual blessings in Christ. (Ephesians 1:3) This is an act of God. God promised blessings even before humans existed ..."For He chose us in him (Christ) before the creation of the world to be holy and blameless in his sight...And he made known to us the mystery of his will...to be put into effect when the times will have reached their fulfillment." (Ephesians 1:4, 10) He predestined believers to become his adopted children through Christ so that they could inherit these blessings. (Ephesians 1:5) There must be a change in our identity and in our spiritual legal status in order for us to have the spiritual legal right to inherit God's blessings. Once we have this right, we can experience these spiritual blessings in the six dimensions of the *newness* of life:

- A new nature: holy and blameless (Ephesians 1:4)
- A new status: as God's adopted sons and daughters (Ephesians 1:5)
- A new start: redemption and forgiveness of sins (Ephesians 1:7)
- A new knowledge: to know the mystery of his will (Ephesians 1:9)
- A new creation: becoming a new man (Ephesians 2:15)
- A new purpose in life: to do good works (Ephesians 2:10)

A New Nature

Holiness and blamelessness were to be the new nature of the believers. To become holy was the prerequisite to overcome the grip of man's sinful nature. The transformation starts within the inner being of the believer. A new nature made in the likeness of the spirit of Christ emerges.

In Chapter 3 on "Wholesome Thinking", I will discuss the transformation of the thinking process that occurs when God calls and separates unto himself "a chosen people, a royal priesthood, a holy nation, a people belonging to God." (1 Peter 2:9) The path to empowerment begins when believers make a separation in their minds of those things which are of God and those things of the world. There is a radical change in the conception of the "self", the world and its value system. In Christ's metaphor, although the believer still lives in the world, the believer does not belong to it. (John 15:19) In this transformation of the conceptual view of the self, the world and its value systems, the believer acquires the new power and the ability to overcome the enslavement of the human self to the power of sin as Paul described it.

Paul wrote in Romans about the struggle within humans' inner being:

> For what I want to do I do not do, but what I hate to do I do. (Romans 7:15)
> For in my inner being I delight in God's law, but I see another law at work in the members of my body, waging war against the law of my mind and making me a prisoner of the law of sin at work within my members. What a wretched man I am! Who will rescue me from this body of death? (Romans 7:22-24)

The conflict Paul described consists of the struggle between two polar opposites: the law of sin[3] embedded in the nature of the "flesh" and the law of God reflected in the Spirit of God. Paul recognized that human nature is basically corrupt, self-centered and powerless to change. To win this struggle in order to attain holiness, one must first overcome the utter helplessness of human nature to give in to the desires of the "flesh". The mind's focus has to shift from doing what human nature naturally desires to do, to doing what is pleasing to God. And for that change in human nature to happen, two events had to occur: First, God had to send "his own Son in the likeness of sinful man to be a sin offering", to destroy the power of sin, so that believers could have the power to live according to what the Spirit desires. (Romans 8:3,5) And second, man had to accept Christ's act through faith to allow the in-dwelling of the Spirit of God. The Spirit of God in the inner being of the believers created the power to change the nature of the human being. Thus, to be empowered in the spirit is to overcome the grip of the desires of the "flesh" through the renewal of the mind to conform to God's standards for behavior.

Having achieved the Spirit of Christ in the inner being, power is then given to continue the process of the renewal of the mind on a daily basis. In a deep spiritual sense, Paul described this process metaphorically as a daily act of death and rebirth— "I die every day." (1 Corinthians 15: 31)—death to sin and alive to God just as the symbolism of baptism suggests when one's old self "dies" during the immersion into the water, and the new "self" emerges during the act of emergence from water. Paul emphasized, "I have been crucified with Christ and I no longer live, but Christ lives in me. The life I live in the body, I live by faith in the Son of God, who loved me and gave himself for me." (Galatians 2:20) One daily lets go of the old habits and desires (Colossians 3:5-9), and acquires new God-like traits. (Colossians 3:12-17) Peter described these traits as consisting of faith, goodness, knowledge, self-control, perseverance, godliness, brotherly kindness and love. (2 Peter 1:5-7) Paul mentioned the fruits of the Spirit as "love, joy, peace, patience, kindness, faithfulness and self-control." (Galatians 5:22-23) And James describes the wisdom that comes from heaven as "pure, peace-loving, considerate, submissive, full of mercy and good fruit, impartial and sincere." (James 3:17) Peter asserts that if one has these qualities in increasing measure, one will attain holiness and blamelessness in the sight of God and will be kept from being ineffective and unproductive in the knowledge of Christ. (2 Peter 1:8) And against such things, Paul said, there is no law. (Galatians 5:23) The Spirit prevails.

A New Status

Believers become the "children of God." "In love, he predestined them to be adopted as his sons through Jesus Christ." (Ephesians 1:5) Believers no longer are aliens to God's kingdom, but are God's children. As children, they are heirs to the glorious inheritance of God. The realization of this new status empowers the mind of the believers not to merely focus on things of this world, but on those things of God.

Those who are led by the Spirit of God are sons of God. (Romans 8:14)
The Spirit himself testifies with our spirit that we are God's children. (Romans 8:16)
You are all sons of God through faith in Christ Jesus, for all of you who were baptized into Christ have clothed yourselves with Christ. (Galatians 3:26-27)

Paul further declared:

If we are children, then we are heirs — heirs of God and co-heirs with Christ, if indeed we share in his sufferings in order that we may also share in his glory. (Romans 8:17)
There is neither Jew nor Greek, slave nor free, male or female, for you are all in Christ Jesus. If you belong to Christ, then you are Abraham's seed, and heirs according to the promise. (Galatians 3:28-29)

This new status gives hope to the believers. It also transforms the meaning of suffering. Suffering becomes bearable and in a spiritual sense, desirable, for it is a path toward the edification of one's faith. (1 Peter 1:6-7) As children of God, believers can hope for the glorious inheritance that is to come. Earthly suffering, compared to the promised spiritual inheritance, is like taking a bitter pill to cure illness. The hope for wellness can sustain a person through periods of pain, trials and suffering. The realization that suffering is temporary because of the promise and hope for a better future is comforting. Believers can share in the suffering of Christ as well as in his glory. A change of attitude towards suffering empowers one to move on while still experiencing difficult and painful circumstances.

God had planned something better for us so that only together with us would they be made perfect. (Hebrews 11:40)

A New Start
One of the most comforting thoughts and privileges of believers is the realization that one can have a fresh start in life in Christ.

In him (Christ), we have redemption through his blood, the
forgiveness of sins, in accordance with the riches of God's
grace. (Ephesians 1:7)

This is something no money can buy. No man can bestow this
grace. It doesn't matter what happened in one's life before. In Christ,
there is a new beginning. God destroyed the power of sin through
the death and resurrection of Christ. A believer in Christ has received
the forgiveness of sins. One does not have to be tied down by all the
guilt, regrets and remorse of past misdeeds. The redemptive power
of Christ forgives all sins. And one can move on to live a new life.
To be redeemed by God through Christ is to empower a person to
start life anew.

God paid a huge price—the blood of Christ— to redeem people.
Although blood sacrifice is something our modern culture may not
understand, the act of redemption through the sacrifice of blood[4]
had been foretold throughout the history of the Jewish people in
Old Testament writings. At the start of their exodus from Egypt, the
blood of the sacrificed lamb was painted on the door frame as a sign
for God to bypass that household and not to strike down their first-
born. (Exodus 12:13) Another example of this foreshadowing of the
blood sacrifice is when Moses instructed the anointed priest of the
Israelites to take the blood of a sacrificed young bull into the Tent of
Meeting as atonement for their sins. (Leviticus 4:14)

Paul said that the acts of sacrifices in the Old Testament and
embodied in the Law of Moses were only a "shadow of the good
things that are coming—not the realities themselves." (Hebrews
10:1) The annual sacrifices as shown in the Old Testament metaphorically foreshadowed the sacrifice of Christ, who as the Messiah,
offered himself as God's sacrificial lamb, once and for all, to redeem
the people to God. Christ was not the symbol any longer but the
reality. (Colossians 2:17) The power that raised Jesus from the dead
was the same power that was available to the believers to start a new
life. Paul prayed:

... that the *eyes of your heart* may be enlightened in order
that you may know the hope to which he has called you,

the riches of his glorious inheritance in the saints, and his incomparable great *power* for us who believe. That *power* is like the working of his mighty strength, which he exerted in Christ when he raised him from the dead. (Ephesians 1:18-19)[5]

Since Christ paid the ultimate price with his blood to redeem sinners, the believers can be relieved of the burden of guilt and sin and can "hold unswervingly to the hope they profess." The believers are saved by grace through the blood sacrifice of Christ. They can experience anew the freedom, power and energy to "spur one another on toward love and good deeds." (Hebrews 10:24)

A New Knowledge

The great mystery of God—to bring all things in heaven and on earth together under one head, Christ, had been revealed to the believers through the apostles. (Ephesians 1:9-10) The mystery of the gospel, salvation through faith in Christ, was preached not to just the Jews but to the gentiles as well. Paul wrote about his insight into the mystery of Christ that was revealed to him. In Christ, he emphasized, the gentiles become co-heirs with Israel to receive the promise of God. (Ephesians 3:6) His grace and mission was to preach the gospel to the gentiles regarding the "unsearchable riches of Christ, and to make plain to everyone the administration of this mystery" through the body of Christ which is the church. (Ephesians 3:8-10)

Paul was the emissary of the gospel to the Gentiles. Furthermore, he explained the spiritual basis of who is a true "Jew" and explicated the process through which believing gentiles were given co-equal status with believing Jews in Christ.

"Through the gospel, the gentiles are heirs together with Israel, members together of one body, and sharers together in the promise of Christ Jesus." (Ephesians 3:6)

Paul emphasized that real change starts from within the individual. The essence of faith is a change of heart, and not just adherence to external laws and rituals as had been practiced in the Mosaic tradition. God's commandment to his people is to be carved in their hearts, and not on stones.

> Hear, O Israel: The Lord our God, the Lord is one. Love the Lord your God with all your heart and with all your soul and with all your strength. These commandments that I give you today are to be upon your *hearts*." (Deuteronomy 6:4-6)

And the covenant God made with the house of Israel will be written in their hearts.

> "This is the covenant I will make with the house of Israel after that time," declared the Lord. "I will put my laws in their minds and write them on their *hearts*. I will be their God, and they will be my people." (Jeremiah 31:33)

The righteousness of God comes through faith in Jesus to all who believe, both to believing Jews and gentiles. (Romans 3:22) A man is a true spiritual Jew, Paul asserted, if he is one inwardly; and that circumcision is circumcision of the heart, by the Spirit, not by the written code. (Romans 2:29) What counts is faith. Paul used the example of Abraham's action to illustrate his faith. Abraham was told by God to leave his homeland to go to a place unknown to him. He took God's word to heart and backed it up with action. When he was about a hundred years old, and his wife Sarah remained child-less, he was unwavering in his belief in God's promise that he will be the "father of many nations." God opened Sarah's womb and gave him a son, Isaac. As a result, he became the Israeli patriarch. Generations of Jews traced their ancestry to him and honored him. He was blessed by God materially and spiritually. Because Abraham was "fully persuaded that God had power to do what he had prom-ised, this is why it (his faith) was credited to him as righteousness." (Romans 4:21-22) Paul summarized the righteousness God bestowed on Abraham this way: "Abraham believed the Lord, and he credited it to him as righteousness." (Genesis 15:6)

In the same manner, Paul explained that the words "it was cred-ited to him" were written not for Abraham alone, but also for *anyone* who believes in God who raised Jesus from the dead for our justifica-tion. (Romans 4:23-24) Thus, God's righteousness will be credited to anyone who believed, as Abraham did, based on God's words.

When God's commandment is firmly established in the believers' heart through faith, the transformation can be profound and powerful. The change of the heart can create a centering of the soul. Believers, individually and collectively, if they truly live up to the tenets of their faith can become powerful, positive influences in the world. The life force and energy that flows from this belief is like a centrifugal force that can emanate concentric waves of energy, first within the individual, then to one's family, further on to one's society, and ultimately to the world. This sequence of the flow of the spheres of influence will be further explained in Chapter 3, Wholesome Thinking.

Paul also revealed the mystery by which the gentiles could be co-heirs with Israel. God had elected Israel as his chosen people. How could gentiles become co-heirs with Israel? Paul explained that the process is akin to grafting a "wild olive branch" into the "orig-inal olive tree." The transgression of Israel, Paul wrote in Romans, leads to the salvation of the gentiles. (Romans 11:11) Gentiles, like a wild olive shoot, are grafted onto the natural olive tree (Israel) where branches have been broken off because of Israel's unbelief. (Romans 11:19-20) This is accomplished through faith, not work, so that no one can boast. Paul wanted the believers to know that this was a mystery God had revealed to him. Just as God initially had hardened the hearts of Pharaoh to forbid the Israelites to leave Egypt to enter Canaan, God has allowed Israel to experience "a hardening *in part* until the full number of the Gentiles has come in." (Romans 11:25) Then Israelites, too, through belief, can be grafted back onto their natural olive tree (Romans 11:23) so that all of Israel will be saved. (Romans 11:26)

This new knowledge allowed believers, Paul wrote, to have direct access to God through the Spirit, to experience God with freedom and confidence, to know that Christ dwelled in their hearts, to be able to be "rooted and established in love", and to grasp the full dimension of the love of Christ so that the believers may be filled to the "measures of all the fullness of God." (Ephesians 3:16-19) This was Paul's prayer and desire for the Ephesians and for all believers. He laid out the path to spiritual maturity, and the new knowledge provided the template to achieve it. This is what the "eyes of the heart" will see.

A New Creation

"His purpose is to create a *new* man out of the two (believers and Christ), thus making peace, and in one body to reconcile both of them to God through the cross, by which he put to death their hostility." (Ephesians 2:15-16) In Christ, a new creation had been formed. Gentiles, once separated far from God, were brought closer to God through the blood of Christ. (Ephesians 2:13) Christ died in the place of sinners. In the sight of God, believers in Christ become "one", united in relationship to their Creator. Christ prayed to the Father, "I in them and you in me." (John 17:23) The barrier that once separated man from God was torn apart when Christ died on the cross. "The curtain of the temple was torn in two." (Luke 23:45) Through one stroke of his supreme sacrifice, Christ made it possible for believers to enter the Holiest of the Holy of the Temple of God. In fact, the believers become "living stones", to be joined together in building the holy temple of the Lord, a dwelling in which God lives with his Spirit. (Ephesians 2:22) The reconciliation with God through Christ brings true peace and inexplicable joy.

This is a profound transformation of the self —a total surrendering of the *self* to conform to God's will. In Christ, the act of new creation empowers believers to become a new person with new character traits. One's lowly body is transformed to be like his glorious body. (Philippians 3: 21) God's will acts through the believers and is the ultimate empowerment. This transformation causes a change in one's beliefs, in how one cares for one's body, in how one cares for and loves others, in how one cares for the environment and in how one learns to become an instrument of peace in the world. And all these miraculous changes begin with the planting of a small mustard seed of faith in the soil of the heart of believers. Paul exclaimed:

Therefore, if anyone is in Christ, he is a new creation; the old has gone, the new has come! (2 Corinthians 5:17)

A New Purpose in Life

"For we are God's workmanship, created in Christ Jesus to do good works, which God prepared in advance for us to do." (Ephesians 2:10) Paul reminded the believers, "The Kingdom of God is not a matter of talk, but of power." (1 Corinthians 4:20) In a psychological sense, Paul described the total transformation of the thought processes, and of the emotions, as shown through actions. Otherwise, believers will live a spiritually schizophrenic existence, with a splitting of intellect from the emotion and behavior. The true test of faith is in actions which I will discuss in Chapter 4, Authentic Life.

In Christ, a tectonic event occurred that shifted the center of gravity from the "self" to "others." Having been created in Christ as the new image of God was like God breathing life into a new clay of man for a new purpose — to live for others and to be God's instrument of righteousness. It seems that God at first separated his people from the world to effect a fundamental change in personality, only to put them back into the world so that they could be positive forces for change. The new creation endowed the believers with a new purpose in life — to do good works. In Christ, believers are empowered to do good deeds. This is their new purpose in life.

Believers now are co-workers with God. Without action, all of Paul's exhortations would have come to nothing if his words had remained just plain "talks." They would have been rationalizations for tolerating misfortune, pain, and the trials of life. They would have been regarded as "projections" of the unconscious mind onto a "religion" of life. They would have become tools for the powerful to use against peace-loving people. They would count for nothing, as faith without deeds is dead. (James 2:26)

Believers' lives are God's work. Each believer has to find the domain of her or his good works. From this position, all the positive forces will emanate out from the believers and will benefit those gathered around. This is life lived to its fullest extent as God has given. Not for selfish gain, but always for the edification of others

47

because in a God-inspired action-oriented life, the Word in us truly becomes flesh.

Power Connection

Christ is the connection to God's great reservoir of spiritual energy. One's spiritual transformation into the full embodiment of a new man happens only *in Christ*. It is through the establishment of a new relationship with God *in Christ* that a new creation can take place. That is why it is likened to the life that flowers when outside branches are grafted onto the vine. Jesus exclaimed, "I am the vine; you are the branches. If a man remains in me and I in him, he will bear much fruit." (John 15:5)

The connection acts like this: First, one's life is grafted onto the vine of Christ through faith. Then, spiritual life is established between the branch and the vine. Finally, life flows within the branch and it will bear fruit. In this way, power flows in the lives of believers because the individual is now connected to God's power source through Christ. Paul explained that God blessed the believers in the heavenly realm with every spiritual blessing in Christ. (Ephesians 1:3) "For no matter how many promises God has made, they are 'Yes' in Christ." (2 Corinthians 1:20)

Just as the great electrical power generated by the Hoover Dam will not help the individual household until the electrical cables to carry it can be brought in, God's vast reservoir of spiritual energy will mean nothing to an individual until a connection is made with God *through* Christ. Christ is God's instrument of change. The Word became flesh and made his dwellings among us. (John 1:14) As a result, the mind, the heart, and the behavior of believers are transformed because of a connection to God through Christ.

Power Generator

The Holy Spirit is a believer's inner generator of spiritual power. "For through him we both have access to the Father by one Spirit." (Ephesians 2:18) In Paul's letter to the Ephesians, he mentioned the roles of the Holy Spirit in at least eight ways (see Chapter 7 for a list of the gifts of the Holy Spirit):

1. The Spirit is the deposit guaranteeing our inheritance until the redemption of those who are God's possession. (Ephesians 1:13-14) God promised the believers will inherit a spiritual inheritance; Christ paid the price for it with the shedding of his blood to seal the promise; and the Spirit provides the "certificate of deposit" that guarantees the realization of the promises of the covenant. Believers do not have to wait till the certificate matures to be assured of God's promise. Spiritual power is always available for those who believe.

2. The Spirit of wisdom and revelation enlightens the eyes of our hearts. (Ephesians 1:17-18; 3:5) God's revelation and mystery are not only a matter of the intellect. The heart has to see and feel it. The Spirit works in mysterious ways to open the mind and heart of those who truly seek God. New insights about God's words can appear in serendipitous ways: meanings revealed; significance understood. Jesus said, "Blessed are the pure in heart, for they will *see* God." (Matthew 5:8) The Spirit reveals God's wisdom to the heart that is ready to see.

3. The Spirit dwells in each individual believer and in the collective body of Christ which is the church. (Ephesians 2:22) Part of the mystery Paul talked about pertains to the spiritual body of Christ which is the church. God intended that through the church the manifold of his wisdom would be made known. (Ephesians 3:10) Believers are the living stones that together build on the foundation of the apostles and prophets, with Christ as the cornerstone. (Ephesians 2:20) As the Israelites built a holy temple so that God could dwell there, so do the present day believers collectively build the holy temple of God in which God dwells by his Spirit.

4. The Spirit promotes unity among the believers. Make every effort to keep the unity of the Spirit through the bond of peace. (Ephesians 4:3) Though there may be as many differences of opinion as there are human beings, the final denominator in the debates and discussions amongst believers should be what is in the best interest and glory of God. And the final arbiter of dissent among believers is the Holy Spirit. This

shows how believers use an entirely different approach to resolve their differences as compared to the methods used by the rest of the world. Believers bring their concerns to the Lord in prayer and ask the Holy Spirit for guidance in resolving conflicts.

5. The Spirit permeates the conscience of the believers. Do not grieve the Holy Spirit of God. (Ephesians 4:30) Believers live with a heightened consciousness of the moral and ethical sensibilities. The standard for behaviors for the believer is the word of God. This demands a higher standard of behavior as compared to those of the world. In fact, believers are to conduct themselves so that their behavior should be unassailable to those who may want to attack them. (1 Peter 2:12) This requires that they shed their habits of bitterness, rage and anger, brawling and slander, envy and malice and other negative character traits. They are to let in the Spirit to bring out kindness and compassion. (Ephesians 4:31-32)

6. The Spirit brings joy. Do not get drunk with wine which leads to debauchery. Instead, be filled with the Spirit. (Ephesians 5:18) The Spirit fills the believer with joy and ecstasy. Such happiness is based on living in a state of grace, of discerning the truths of God, in the realization of faith and understanding the mystery of Christ, in the glorious hope for the spiritual blessings of God stored in Christ, and in doing God's will. It is the working of the Spirit and it does not rely on anything artificial like wine or stimulants.

7. The Spirit of truth is the word of God. "Take the helmet of salvation and the sword of the Spirit which is the Word of God." (Ephesians 6:17) The Spirit of God will impart confidence of God's truth in the believers and will guide the believer to confront different ideologies in the world. Paul told the Ephesians that their fight is against the forces of evil in this world and that their weapon is the word of God. Christ set the example when he was tempted by the devil. He overcame temptation by using the words of God.[6] In like manner, believers should understand the scriptures as the revealed

word of God. Such knowledge will empower them to resist temptation and to fight a winning ideological battle.

8. The Spirit strengthens believers to proclaim the gospel of Christ. Paul asked the Ephesians to pray for him: "Pray for me, that whenever I open my mouth, words may be given so that I will fearlessly make known the mystery of the gospel." (Ephesians 6:19) Prayer moves the heart of God. Prayer also connects the bond of those who believe. Prayer enables things to happen. No wonder even a strong and stalwart warrior of Christ like Paul asked for prayer for spiritual sustenance to fearlessly proclaim the gospel. The Spirit buoys a believer when no other means can.

Power Switch

Faith is the switch that turns on the generator that brings in God's spiritual power. Through belief in the gospel of salvation, believers become the children of God and are heirs to the spiritual inheritance mentioned above.

You also were included in Christ when you heard the word of truth, the gospel of your salvation. Having *believed*, you were marked in him with a seal, the promised Holy Spirit, who is a deposit guaranteeing our inheritance until the redemption of those who are God's possession—to the praise of his glory. (Ephesians 1:13-14)

Paul prayed that through faith, Christ may dwell in the hearts of believers and will strengthen their inner beings through the Spirit. (Ephesians 3:16-17) Like the life that is stored in a mustard seed, it will not germinate until it comes in contact with the soil of faith. In like manner, God's power can be accessed through faith. It is a simple design, but elegant.

Power Current

Love is God's spiritual power current. It is the distinguishing feature that often separates the lives of the believer from others. It is also the power that can be used to influence the world. In love, there is the fulfillment of the greatest commandment of God that Jesus affirmed:

> Love the Lord your God with all you heart and with all your soul and with all your mind and with all your strength. Love your neighbor as yourself. (Mark 12:29-31)

Paul prayed specifically for the Ephesians:

> And I pray that you, being rooted and established in love, may have power, together with all the saints, to grasp how wide and long and high and deep is the *love* of Christ, and to know this *love* that surpasses knowledge—that you may be filled to the measure of all the fullness of God. (Ephesians 3:17-19)

When the Spirit empowers the inner being of believers, God's love naturally will flow through their lives. Peter describes this transformational process as being akin to a newborn baby naturally craving spiritual milk. (1 Peter 2:2) By living out the love of Christ in one's life, the believer gets to taste and know the full dimension of the love of Christ and to gain an understanding of the measure of the fullness of God.

Power Manifestations

The connection with Christ brings power. And that power is manifested in the lives of believers in the fullest sense: their thinking process, feelings and emotions[7], behavior and all other aspects of their relationships are changed. Being made "alive with Christ" (Ephesians 2:5), believers are urged to live their lives for God in these following six manners:

1. *Live a life worthy of the calling one has received.* (Ephesians 4:1)

    The attitudes of the "new man in Christ" are ones of humility and gentleness, patience, and "bearing with one another in love." One makes "every effort to keep the unity of the Spirit through the bond of peace." Dissension is to be avoided. One may differ with another's opinion, but every effort is to be made to reconcile and compromise for the *sake* of Christ.

The idea is that all believers, as living stones, need to contribute to building the holy temple of God, "built on the foundation of the apostles and prophets, with Christ himself as the chief cornerstone." That means each individual utilizes one's talents, through works of service, and contributes by working together to build the spiritual body of Christ. The Spirit binds the faithful in a harmonious way and in love. It is in works of service that one gains increasing knowledge of Christ and grows into full spiritual maturity. (Ephesians 4:12-13)

2. *Live as Children of light.* (Ephesians 4:17-32)

Believers are to put off the "old self" and put on the "new self." The old self acts according to the desires of the flesh; the new self thinks, feels, and acts according to the new way of God. As children of God, they acquire new attitudes of the mind. These new attitudes are manifested as behavioral traits in daily life, including a greater sensibility to others, an improved way of speaking, management of anger, a new attitude towards work, and in the emotional life overall.

In speech: speak truthfully to another; say only what is helpful to others.

In anger: do not sin; do not hold the day's anger till sunset.

In work: do not steal; do something useful to share with others.

In feelings: be kind and compassionate. (Ephesians 4:25-32)

3. *Live a life of love.* (Ephesians 5:1)

Imitate Christ's sacrificial love. The lifestyle of believers should not be greedy, self-centered or hurtful to others. In this context, as God's holy people, it is only proper that the conduct of believers be pure, moral, and honest. The ethics of their behavior should be above reproach. In fact, their standards of behavior are such that they are to have no hint of sexual immorality, of any kind of impurity, or of greed or foolish talk. (Ephesians 5:3-4) Not only are believers to act accordingly, they are to dissociate themselves from those who commit such acts.

4. *Live wisely.* (Ephesians 5:15)

Time is precious and the days are full of evil. To accomplish their new purpose in life, believers need to cultivate good time management skills. God's business assumes priority. They need to understand God's will, and be filled with the Holy Spirit. The joy of a new life bubbles forth with singing and making music. One feels thankful to God for everything.

5. *Live out of reverence for Christ.* (Ephesians 5:21)

In all relationships where there is a difference in the axes of power and authority, submit to one another out of *reverence for Christ.* (Ephesians 5:21) There is a keen awareness of a reciprocal relationship because of the presence of Christ. In the Christian encounter between two individuals, there are actually three persons involved: the other person, one self, and Christ. Paul brought out the beauty of such interactions in three common relationships where there is a difference in the axis of power:

a. Between husbands and wives

The analogy Paul used for this relationship was the relationship between Christ and the church. Christ is the head of his body, the church. Christ loved the church and died for her. In the same manner, husbands are to love their wives as they love themselves. Wives are to respect their husbands and honor them. For in Christ, husbands and wives are united in "one flesh."

This new marital relationship left no ground for chauvinism, for abuse of any kind, or selfishness. The difference in this new relationship was that out of *reverence for Christ,* one must adjust towards a new equality, reciprocity, and caring for one another. There was to be bliss in the marital relationship with Christ as the central bond.

b. Between children and parents

As Christ obeyed and honored the Father, children were to honor their parents. This commandment promised a long life. (Deuteronomy 5:16)

Parents should love their children as the Father loved his Son. There are many ways parents can show their love for their children. But in discipline, there is no need to provoke a child to anger. Children should be brought up in the "training and instruction of the Lord." (Ephesians 6:4)

c. Between slaves and masters

Slavery, prevalent at the time of the apostles, now has been abolished in many parts of the world. What replaced that relationship in our discussion of current relationships is the difference in authority between the employer and the employee. Out of reverence for Christ, both employers and employees are to relate in egalitarian terms in the eyes of God. This changes their attitude toward work and their treatment of each other. Although authority is not relinquished, and both parties continue to discharge their responsibilities in their respective roles, there is a whole new attitude of serving, working, and relating. Employees are to obey their employers as they would Christ with a genuine sincerity of heart and respect. Employees are to diligently attend to work not only in the presence of their employers and to please them, but with a diligence that stems from a belief in doing God's will at work. Believers enjoy the freedom that is in Christ and they perform willingly and wholeheartedly as if serving the Lord.

In similar spirit, employers should not exploit their employees. God is impartial. The payment of wages and privileges should be fair. Out of reverence for Christ, employers should regard employees with due respect. Employers carry out their responsibilities not just out of duty, but out of love. Their employees are co-believers in Christ. Although each has a different role and set of responsibilities, in this new relation in Christ, there is equality of status in the sight of God.

6. *Towards systems of power and instruments of evil*

Having been empowered by God, how should the believer act towards the forces of evil? Does the transformation of the self to conform to the image of Christ mean that believers should be passive and bystanders in the affairs of the world? Does "not belonging to the world" mean a retreat to asceticism? Not so, Paul admonished, "Be strong in the Lord and in his mighty power. Put on the full armor of God to take a stand against the devil's scheme. For our struggle is not against flesh and blood, but against the rulers, against the authorities, against the powers of this dark world, and against the spiritual forces of evil in the heavenly realms." (Ephesians 6:10-12) Since the struggle is in the spiritual realm, believers should arm themselves with the full spiritual battle gear to fight against the forces of evil. Evil may be found in the individual, systemic, ideological, or cultural arena. Believers are exhorted to be on guard and to stand firm in their faith. Paul's metaphor of "putting on the full armor of God" carries rich spiritual meanings. Here are my thoughts:

1. Belt of truth: Truthfulness must be the defining character of a believer. In truth, there is strength. Because the accountability of the believer is ultimately to God who has called her or him out of darkness to enter into the kingdom of light, the believer's mind, heart and soul should be constantly attuned to the pitch of God, as the strings of a precious violin respond to the touch of its master.

> Search me, O God, and know my heart,
> Test me and know my anxious thoughts.
> See if there is any offensive way in me,
> And lead me in the way everlasting.
> (Psalms 139:23-24)

This prayer of the psalmist should be every believer's prayer.

The believer who does not adhere to the truth or speaks falsehood, or worse, manipulates the truth to suit one's purpose, becomes a hypocrite, something that Jesus abhorred. Authenticity of character must be at the core of the personality of a true believer. This doesn't mean at all times one has to blurt out an honest opinion regardless of the context of the conversation or the readiness of the hearer to hear, but that the believer must be truthful to oneself, to others, and to God.

2. Breastplate of righteousness. The breastplate is used to protect the part of the body where the heart is. The heart of the believer should be righteous. While one may not always be taking the popular position, one must be willing to take a stand for what is right. Jesus said, "Blessed are those who are persecuted because of righteousness, for theirs is the kingdom of heaven." (Matthew 5:10)

3. Feet fitted with readiness for peace. Believers should be the messengers and instruments of peace. The peace that comes from the grace of God should be manifested in the lives of the believers. Christ is the ultimate model of peace-making because he offered himself up as atonement for the sins of men so that man could be reconciled to God. In like manner, believers are to be the reconciler of conflict. Their task is to spread the gospel of peace. Christ preached to the multitudes:

Blessed are the peacemakers, for they will be called sons of God. (Matthew 5:9)

The words of the prophet Micah regarding peace were etched into a monument that now stands at the entrance to the United Nations building in New York City:

They will beat their swords into plowshares
and their spears into pruning hooks.
Nation will not take up sword against nation,
Nor will they train for war anymore. (Micah 4:3)

Where there is the gospel of Christ, there is peace.

4. Shield of faith. Standing firm in one's faith is the best protection against the flaming arrows of the evil ones. (Ephesians 6:16) A believer's faith needs to be rooted in the words of God so that one can withstand those conflicting ideologies that may undermine one's faith. The battleground for the control of the mind is fought within and outside the church. Outside, the gospel is constantly being challenged by ideologies of the secular world. Inside, as both Peter and Paul had warned, false prophets preach heresies in the church. Being clearly grounded in the scriptural truths armed the believers then with the discerning power to distinguish truth from false-hood, so their faith could be steadfastly anchored on the rock of Christ's teachings.

5. Helmet of salvation. Believers put on this helmet of salvation in order to distinguish themselves as belonging to God and to protect their minds from the words of lawless men. At the same time, the gospel of salvation is proclaimed and God's transforming power of salva-tion is witnessed in the lives of the believers. In words and in actions, believers become the salt and light of the world. Salt, for the essence of the transformed life and one's character provides seasoning for others. Light, for they live the truth and bring good deeds to the people they come in contact with. Peter urged believers to set apart Christ in their hearts, so that they are always prepared with an answer to anyone who asks for a reason for the hope that they have. (1 Peter 3:15)

6. Sword of the Spirit. The word of God is the "sword" that both convicts and converts. Since the battle is in a spiritual realm, God's words need to be proclaimed so that all men

can come to the realization of the truth and the salvation God has prepared for those He called.

In the beginning was the Word, and the Word was with God and the word was God. (John 1:1)

The Word became flesh and made his dwelling among us. (John 1:14)

To all who received him, to those who believed in his name, he gave the right to become the children of God. (John 1:12)

Thus, Paul urged believers "to put on the full armor of God" and "be strong in the Lord and in his mighty power." (Ephesians 6:10-11)

Discussion and Summary

I used Paul's metaphor of the "eyes of the heart" to explore his spirituality. Paul's spirituality is reflected in his profound insight into God and Christ as revealed to him following his conversion and in his understanding of how one can obtain this transforming power. He pointed to the strengthening of the inner being of the believers as the path to obtain spiritual power. Like the need for electrical energy to run the necessities of modern life, we need spiritual energy to meet the challenges we face in our lives today. The key spiritual issue we face is the utter helplessness to change patterns of human behavior. We see this pervasive helplessness around us and in us: in the struggles of mental patients to overcome their emotional problems; among church members who are lukewarm and won't practice what they learned; among clergy who have committed sexual abuse; in evangelists who led lives that are contrary to what they preach; among politicians who abused their power and behave in ways that crossed the moral boundary line and are helpless to overcome their character defects; and in our difficulties to change our patterns of living to achieve a healthier life. Paul wanted the believers to obtain this inner source of strength. And he laid out his thinking in his letter to the Ephesians.

Since the feeling of helplessness is like a house that is gradually deprived of electrical energy, I thought the analogy of the field of electrical energy dynamics would be an apt description of our emotional state and decided to use the analogy to organize and explain Paul's description of how to overcome our helplessness and to obtain this powerful spiritual life.

Paul wanted us to focus first on the interiority of our inner being and to obtain spiritual power in Christ to overcome this helplessness. That change must start first within the core of our being. He showed us how to tap into this vast reservoir of God's energy field through faith in God and in his son Jesus Christ and to invite the in-dwelling of the Holy Spirit. This is the secret to Christian spirituality and empowerment and in this chapter I tried to lay out Paul's conception of the changes in one's thinking, emotions and actions that may occur in the lives of the believers. This change does not affect the intellect alone. Christian spirituality involves the total transformation of the heart, mind and actions to conform to what the Lord desires. (Jeremiah 17:10) Viewing the change from an anthropological perspective, we could say that the transformation that Paul described involved changes in the whole subjective culture of the mind—concepts and percepts, propositions (ways in which the concepts and percepts are related), values, beliefs, and operational procedures (ways of accomplishing things)—to conform to Christ's and God's standards for behavior. Paul explained that this transformational process is achieved through an *identification with Christ* through belief. The result of this change would transform our self-centered culture to a God-centered and other-person-oriented culture. This inner empowerment will lead to a powerful spiritual life.

"As the Spirit indwells, the heart will be led to see where it wants to go."

- *Albert C. Gaw, M.D.*

KEY POINTS:

- St. Paul's metaphor of the "eyes of the heart" is explicated as a way to understand Christian spirituality.

- The analogy of electric power dynamics is used to examine the meaning of the *power* theme in the book of Ephesians.

- God has a *power* plan for us.

- God's power plan includes six dimensions of a *new* life:

  - A new nature that is holy
  - A new status as God's adopted children.
  - A new start with the redemption of life and the forgiveness of sins.
  - A new understanding of God's mystery.
  - A new creation in becoming a new man.
  - A new purpose in life to do good deeds.

- God's plan is actualized through a faith in Christ.

- The Holy Spirit which comes to dwell in the believers empowers them to overcome the weaknesses of their human nature and to change their character to conform to God's nature. The Holy Spirit performs at least the following eight functions for the believers:

  - Assuring them that they will receive their spiritual inheritance.
  - Receiving the revelation of God's mystery.
  - Partaking in the building of the spiritual body of God.
  - Promoting unity.
  - Heightening their conscience.
  - Bringing joy and happiness.
  - Guiding them to understand the word of God.
  - Emboldening them to proclaim the gospel of Christ.

- Love is the Christian's signal spiritual *power current*.

- The "fruits" of a powerful Christian spiritual life are manifested in a *changed* life and are manifested in the following ways:

  - Living a life worthy of one's calling.
  - Living as children of light.
  - Living a life of love.
  - Living wisely.
  - Living out of reverence for Christ.
  - Living as instruments of righteousness against the power of evil in this world.

- Believers are urged to be on guard and stand firm in their faith and put on the "full armor of God" and put on the following spiritual gear:

  - The belt of truth.
  - The breastplate of righteousness.
  - Feet fitted with readiness for peace.
  - The shield of faith.
  - The helmet of salvation.
  - The sword of the Spirit.

3. Peter: Wholesome Thinking

SIGNIFICANCE:

Cultivate wholesome thinking. It will empower you to live your life on a higher plain.

Peter

"Dear friends, this is my second letter to you. I have written both of them as reminders to stimulate you to *wholesome thinking*." (2 Peter 3:1)

Introduction

In contrast to Paul whose conversion was dramatic, Peter's spirituality unfolded gradually. Peter was a fisherman when Christ called him to be a disciple. That he became a leader of Christ's twelve apostles entrusted with carrying on the mission of Christ and his teachings is, in itself, a miraculous transformation of character. When Christ called him, he never hesitated and he never looked back. For three years, he witnessed first-hand many activities of Christ's and learned his teachings. Like the initial reaction of many who were called to follow Christ, Peter doubted Christ's identity, particularly the claim that he is the Son of God. Eventually, he came to a deep realization and conviction that Jesus was indeed who he claimed to be. But the transformation of his beliefs regarding Christ, unlike the dramatic conversion of Saul on the road to Damascus, was gradual. Peter had to be led and shown, so it seems, until he could admit that "You are the Christ, the Son of the living God."(Matthew 16:16) He had to undergo three denials of Christ for him to realize that Christ wanted him to "feed my lambs." (John 21:15) His personal faith was tested through trials and tribulations. After Christ's departure, Peter assumed a key leadership role in the church in Jerusalem. (Acts 15:6-11) It was Peter, responding to a vision from God, who preached to Cornelius, a Roman Centurion at Caesarea that opened the door of the gospel to the Gentiles. (Acts 10:1-48)

Peter did not write much. But these two letters (1 and 2 Peter) addressed to the early Christians scattered in Asia Minor (Pontus, Galatia, Cappadocia, Asian and Bithynia), were attributed to him. At the time he wrote them, he knew he wouldn't live much longer. It also was a trying and dangerous time for all the believers. Outwardly, the Christians faced persecution by Emperor Nero. Inwardly, the faithful whom the apostles had painstakingly nurtured, faced competing ideologies and heretic teachings that threatened to undermine their faith in Jesus Christ. Peter felt an urgency to encourage the believers to stand firm in their faith. He sensed that there was a struggle for the mind of the believers. To Peter, it seems that winning the battle of the mind was far more important than just safeguarding the physical body. For believers to remain steadfast in their faith, their beliefs must be anchored in the words of the prophets and of Christ. Thus, he challenged them to recall the words spoken in the past by the holy prophets and the words of Christ spoken through his disciples. (2 Peter 3:2) He reminded them that he was writing with authority and as a first-hand witness of the transfiguration of Christ on the mountain. And he wrote these two epistles (letters) to stimulate them to wholesome thinking. What do "the eyes of the heart" of Peter see?

Wholesome thinking

First Peter

The American Heritage Dictionary defines "wholesome" as "conducive to sound health or well-being." To think is "to reason about or reflect on; ponder."[1] Thus, Peter wanted the believers to reflect on the teachings they received so that their spiritual health would remain strong. But as Peter expounded on aspects of wholesome thinking, he did not just sketch the contour of the tree trunk of faith; he actually painted the full panorama of Christian living. He laid out the entire pathway, including all the rocks and hurdles that may come along the way, to reach a deep, mature Christian spiritual life. He explained to the believers who they are, their new identity, their purpose in living, the meaning of suffering, and their hope for the future. Thus, Peter's exigency addressed the fundamental questions that have confronted mankind since time immemorial: where do we come from, where are we going, what is the meaning of suffering, is there life after death, and how should we live? In short, Peter's letters focused on the basic questions of the meaning of human existence and provided clear answers from a Christian perspective. Thus, Peter's epistles can also be regarded as an exposition of the Christian philosophy of living. In this context, I explicate first what Peter meant by wholesome thinking and how to acquire it and then I show the implications of that for a Christian philosophy of living.

The words of the disciples

What did the disciples preach? Peter suggested that the central tenet of their message was that God is the prime mover, the author of the Christian faith and that the believers, through a belief in Christ, become a "chosen people, a royal priesthood, a holy nation, a people belonging to God." (1 Peter 2:9) These new Christian identities seemed to connote four different but inter-related phases in the transformation of the self. They also suggested a trajectory of the effects of a spiritual transformation that starts with a subjective change within the innermost being of the individual's personality, and leads to the believers becoming collectively a powerful, positive force for change in the world. The ultimate destiny of this inner journey is for the believer to reach the glorious goal of the salvation of their soul. (1 Peter 1:9) This change in the identity and the new way of thinking of a believer is what Peter meant by "wholesome thinking." Let us consider what these four stages connote:

1. A chosen people. Both Peter and Paul emphasized that God chose and separated out a group of people to be called His own. Once a person's spiritual citizenship changed to God's, he or she becomes an *alien* or *stranger* in the world. (1 Peter 2:9-11; Ephesians 1:4-5)

2. A royal priesthood. The calling initiates in the mind of the believer a questioning of the existing value system and to separate "things of God and things of the world." (1 Peter 2:9; Ephesians 4:22-23) By adopting God's values, a believer starts to "purify" oneself by getting rid of worldly values.
3. A holy nation. Believers act according to God's criteria of holiness. This includes the power to reject activities that seek fulfillment of the "flesh." Rather, believers' personalities take on characteristics described as the "fruits" of the spirit.
4. A people of God. Believers now act according to God's will and seek to do things that please God. (Ephesians 5:10)

These shifts in the mindset of the believer represent a radical transformation of the self. Recalling the words of Christ, although Christians are still in this world, they no longer belong. (John 15:19; 17:14) The transformation is reflected in the change of one's perception, thinking and feeling towards existing societal values. One's value system begins to be shaped by God's words. A new meaning for existence is formed that is reflected in a new philosophy of living. (The processes of change in the mind of the believer will be elaborated later.)

Peter reminded them that it is through the enduring words of the gospel that God has given them *a new birth* into a *living hope*. (1 Peter 1:3) "The Word became flesh and made his dwelling among us." (John 1:14) Jesus prayed to the Father, "I gave them the words you gave me and they accepted them." (John 17:8) The new birth is a spiritual act of being born into the family of God through a belief in the power of the resurrected Christ. Believers, being new persons belonging to a new order of God, are privileged to become God's chosen people. And because they now become the children of God, they are entitled as heirs to their glorious inheritance in heaven. That is the living hope of the Christian—to receive the goal of their faith—the salvation of their souls. That is the "grace that was to come." The prophets have spoken about this state of grace and have long searched for the timing and circumstances of this salvation. Even angels long to know. But the privilege of knowing was revealed two thousand years ago to the disciples who preached the gospel both to the Jews and the gentiles. And what a privilege the early Christians had! The realization of it gives joy and praise to God. With the glorious inheritance that is to come, earthly suffering and persecutions pale in comparison. For this reason, their faith as an example becomes a bulwark against suffering. For God's mercy is more than sufficient to strengthen and sustain them through their periods of trials and tribulations.

Suffering takes on a whole new meaning. It no longer is something to be avoided. On the contrary, Peter said that suffering is the flame of God that tests and purifies one's faith so that its quality will be as pure gold. (1 Peter 1:7) Having purified one's faith, the mind is now ready for action.

Preparing the mind for action

Chosen of God

With the realization of a new birth into a living hope, Peter urged Christians to prepare their minds for action. (1 Peter 1:13) Faith without action is dead. (James 2:26) The action starts with those changes within the personality of the believers such as their attitudes, emotions, identity and behavior. This process of spiritual transformation is a gradual, daily, life-long process of renewal and re-working of human character to conform to that of Christ's and to acquire God-like qualities. It is a daily spiritual experience of "death" to the flesh and the world, but alive in the "spirit" and to God. Paul aptly expressed it when he said, "I died daily." (1 Corinthians 15:31) "For to me to live is Christ, and to die is gain." (Philippians 1:21)

This cognitive transformation brings a new source of spiritual strength through the indwelling of the Holy Spirit. The coming of the Holy Spirit was promised by Jesus before he died. (John 16:7) "It is for your good that I am going away. Unless I go away, the Counselor will not come to you; but if I go, I will send him to you." (John 16:17) The Holy Spirit becomes the new source of strength to overcome old patterns of behavior or character traits. "Old" character traits that belong to the "flesh" are to be shed like old clothes. And Christians are to acquire a new set of "God-like" character traits and to behave differently. The transforming power of the Holy

Spirit enables a believer to live a life different from the prevailing values, ideologies, beliefs and actions of the present "world." This is the power of belief. Belief initiates a process of change—a willingness to examine what is "good" or "bad" for one's life; a strengthening of the "will" to do what's right and beneficial to oneself and others; a desire to seek an existence that has meaning and that brings lasting happiness and satisfaction; an opportunity to experience a new range of emotions such as peace, love, joy and hope; and a way to find the energy and motivation to overcome life's challenges. The act of believing becomes a new power source because of this connection to God's huge spiritual energy field. In Chapter 2, I described how that process of empowerment can happen when one believes in Christ.

A Royal Priesthood

The renewal of the mind in order to act calls for self-edification. "Sanctified them by the truth; your word is truth." (John 17: 17) Sanctification is a prerequisite for one who is called to God's service. Peter exhorted the Christians to be holy as God is holy. (1 Peter 1:16) Just as the Levites in the Old Testaments were called and separated from other Israelites and had to purify and consecrate themselves to devote themselves wholly to God's service and to serving others (Leviticus 11:44-45, 19:2, 20:7; Numbers 8:6,14), Christians, as new "priests" of God, also must attain "holiness" in order to serve. The process of achieving holiness, as noted earlier, requires the abandonment of old habits and the acquisition of new ones. It means ridding oneself of evil desires and focusing one's mind on the hope for the grace of God. It is an act of spiritual purification. Once purified, then Christians are in a position to implement the supreme spiritual act of worship—the offering of one's body as living sacrifice, holy and pleasing to God. (Romans 12:1) This is the status of *royal priesthood*. Unlike during the times of the Old Testament when the perennial sacrifices of unblemished animals in the temple of God was required for the atonement of sins, Christ paid the supreme sacrifice once and for all when he offered himself as God's sacrificial lamb. He was the High Priest that paved the way for believers to attain "royal priesthood" and provided the template for holy living. Because Christ paid the ultimate price — His precious blood (1 Peter 1:19) — the believers can, in response to this love of God's, and out of gratitude and reverent fear, reciprocate that sentiment by offering their "unblemished self" to God.

A Holy Nation

All believers who have sanctified themselves now are citizens of the Holy Nation of God. Its preamble and credo is *love*. Being born again through the enduring word of God, and becoming purified by obeying the truth, an emotional change occurs that generates a new capacity for loving. This will be reflected in a change of personality traits. Believers are to have "sincere love for their brothers, and to love one another deeply, from the heart." (1 Peter 1:22)

The behavioral change calls for ridding oneself of all malice and deceit, hypocrisy, envy, and slander. Being "born into" the new kingdom of God will transform the believers' value system and attitudes and imbue them with a new capacity to love. Like new born babies, believers will naturally crave pure, spiritual milk which is the word of God. They will also have the innate capacity to develop, grow and mature into the fullness of a new spiritual being, described as achieving "the full dimension of salvation." As new citizens of the new kingdom they will acquire character traits that were explicated later by Peter in his second epistle.

People of God

Simultaneously, the act of self-purification also means the preparation of the believer's mind to participate in building the community of God. Action is required. In a spiritual sense, each believer becomes a "living stone" and contributes to the building of a collective, invisible, spiritual house of God, in which spiritual sacrifices are offered acceptable to God through Jesus Christ. (1 Peter 2:4-5) But they also participate in the building of the visible body of Christ, the church, where there is a communion of like-minded people, sharing the culture of God, doing good deeds for the glory of God, and benefiting all mankind. Thus, believers collectively as people of God become the instruments of God to create positive changes in the world.

This then is my sense of what Peter meant when he summed up the glorious new status of the believers—"You are a chosen people, a royal priesthood, a holy nation, a people belonging to God." (1 Peter 2:9)

The action plan for the new mind

Reminded of their new status, Peter urged Christians to make a real difference in their lives in terms of the ways they related to others and to the world. This is the essence of Christian living. Here, Peter used the word "live" four times in 1 Peter and once at the end of 2 Peter to emphasize the changes in attitudes and in relationships and to encourage those actions that should flow from this new mindset:

1. *Live a good life.* (1 Peter 2:12) Not for self-indulgence but for others. One should strive to live a life that is as morally and ethically impeccable as possible. The good deeds of the believers are to be so transparent that they can withstand any wrongful accusation lodged against them by non-believers. (1 Peter 3:16) Peter set the standard when he says: "Live such good lives among the pagans that, though they accuse you of doing wrong, they may see your good deeds and glorify God on the day he visits us." (1 Peter 2:12)

2. *Live as free men and as servants of God.* (1 Peter 2:16) Believers are to show respect to everyone, love their brothers and sisters, fear God, and honor the ruler. Although they are subjected to outside, worldly authority; inwardly, believers are to live as free men and as servants of God. The freedom in Christ is not a license for self-indulgence or a cover-up for evil, or for abuse of power. Rather, it provides opportunities to express one's virtues and to perform good deeds.

   As I have explained in Chapter 2, out of respect for Christ, a change happens in the perception of ones' relationships and one's roles in them, particularly where an inherent difference in *axes* of power and authority occurs in the structure of such relationships. Peter singled out the four common relationships that have differences in *axes* of power and authority: slave/master, wives/husbands, young people/elders, and parishioners/ church elders. (See also Chapter 2) Since both Peter and Paul were contemporary, it is not surprising that Peter might have shared some ideas that Paul had preached. However, Peter, the shepherd of God's flock, added an explanation of what a pastoral relationship between church leaders and parishioners should be like.

Slaves and Masters

Out of *reverence for Christ*, a new attitude emerged in the interaction between slaves and masters in ancient times. Using the same analogy, there should be an attitude of equality between employees and employers in the contemporary work place that stems from an inner freedom and choice brought about by the spirit of Christ. This new attitude about work includes doing one's job to please God not just earthly bosses. God is the "real boss" and one serves always as though one is serving God. This applies to both the employers and employees. From God's perspective, both parties of believers are his children. Peter said that serving and suffering for doing good and out of a new consciousness of God are commendable. (1 Peter 2:19) Christ himself set the example by the way he served the Father by willingly dying on the cross for sinners. Hence, a new willingness and joy in mutual serving develops because both employees and employers, as believers, are serving God through their diligence at work.

Wives and Husbands

As I explained in Chapter 2, Paul's assertion that where in a marital relationship the central bond is a respect for Christ, the attitude of the couple towards each other will be reciprocal and equal. Neither one should desire controlling or subjugating the other; rather, both should show mutual respect and love. Both Paul and Peter advised that wives should submit to their husbands. And if a husband is an unbeliever, his wife, through her purity and reverence and the "unfading inner beauty of a quiet and gentle spirit" (1 Peter 3:4), manifested in action, may win him over to the word.

A husband should love his wife as Christ loved the church and was willing to die for her. Peter mentioned an added bonus: for a husband who is considerate and treats his wife with respect, there is a clear path to effective prayer and spirituality. (1 Peter 3:7)

Young People and Elders

Young people should be humble and be submissive to elders and be alert and exercise self-controlled. (1 Peter 5:5,8) By respecting their elders, their reverence for Christ will also be reflected.

Parishioners and Church Elders

Church elders, those in the church who assume offices as overseers, are to be shepherds of God's flock, not because they must, but because they will; not due to greed for money, but because they are eager to serve; not lording it over others entrusted to their care, but being an example to the flock. Christ, the Chief Shepherd, set the example. The reward of good stewardship is an "everlasting crown of glory." (1 Peter 5: 2-4)

3. *Live in harmony.* (1 Peter 3:8). All believers are to live in harmony, love as brothers, and be compassionate and humble. "Do not repay evil with evil, or insult with insult, but with blessings." (1 Peter 3:9) Set Christ apart in one's heart and keep a clear conscience. Always be prepared "to give an answer to everyone who asks you to give the reason for the hope that you have. But do this with gentleness and respect." (1 Peter 3:15)

4. *Live for the will of God.* (1 Peter 4:2) Live no more for evil human desires. Abandon the desires of the flesh. People with whom one used to associate with may think it strange that believers no longer wanted to partake anymore in any form of evil behavior. As a result, believers may even be abused. Thus, believers should arm themselves for suffering with the

same attitude as Christ, who had suffered in the body and was done with sin. (1 Peter 4:1)

Attitudinal change towards suffering

Be Clear Minded (1 Peter 4:7)

As mentioned earlier, suffering was real to the early Christians and took on a new meaning. Outwardly, they faced persecution by the authorities, sanctioned by the Emperor Nero. They even experienced abuse by those whom they had formerly known. Peter exhorted them to be *clear minded* because the end of all things was near and to exercise self-control so that they could pray and love each other deeply. Armed with Christ's attitude, these believers rejoiced during the painful trials of suffering, for they knew that they were participating in the suffering of Christ. Their thinking was clear—to suffer for doing good deeds was to identify with Christ and experience his suffering.

So then, those who suffer according to God's will should commit themselves to their faithful Creator and continue to do good. (1 Peter 4:19)

Peter ended his first letter by reminding the believers that suffering is transient. The God of all grace will restore them and make them strong, firm and steadfast. Therefore, believers ought to stand fast in the true grace of God. (1 Peter 5:12)

2 Peter

Peter's second letter opened with a reminder that God's power gave believers all they needed for life and that through the knowledge of God "who called them by his own glory and goodness" they would know godliness. (2 Peter 1:3) God calls; God gives; God empowers. In Christ, the believers received faith, hope and power. The path of faith when tested, leads to holiness. Just as the faith of the Israelites had to be tried during their passage through the desert after they left Egypt, a Christian's faith needs to be tested to grow in the world. For Christians to partake in divine nature and escape the corruption of the flesh caused by evil desires, one's faith needs to undergo a process of spiritual transformation.

Peter admonished the believers to acquire sequential virtues:

Add to your faith, goodness; and to goodness, knowledge; and to knowledge; self-control; and to self-control, perseverance; and to perseverance, godliness; and to godliness, brotherly kindness; and to brotherly kindness, love. (2 Peter 1:5-7)

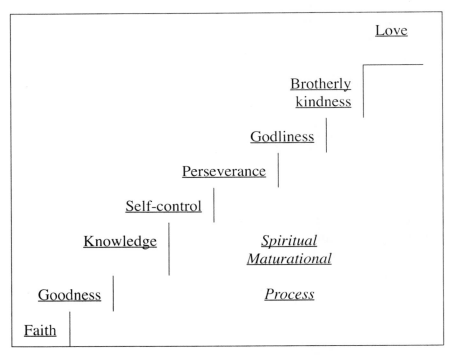

Figure 1. Stages of Spiritual Maturation

Source: 2 Peter 1:5-7

He seems to be suggesting that there is an upward trajectory of spiritual growth. I believe it is useful to conceptualize spiritual growth as a series of stages of development akin to stages of physical and emotional growth. A new birth in Christ means spiritual cells have to differentiate and grow into a new, unique, mature God-like human person. At the time of a spiritual birth, the potential to develop into a glorious spiritual being is present. But a supportive environment for growth is also vitally important. The new believer needs to experience warmth and consistency in the responses of fellow believers to validate the "faith" that binds them together and that will bring about a new experience of life.

Furthermore, the development and attainment of God-like characteristics necessitate a predetermined trajectory of spiritual growth. The trajectory may not necessarily follow a fixed linear direction as shown in Figure 1. In real life, more often than not, one's spiritual development may encounter peaks and valleys so that the trajectory may resemble more a spiral growth, with advances and retreats. Nevertheless, the overall direction is an elevation and enrichment of the character traits of the individual's personality. The highest point is reached when one can transcend parochial sentiment, as Christ showed, and be able to love every one, even one's enemy. At the highest level of a Christian spiritual life, one becomes more tolerant, more sensitive and inclusive of others, and can perceive and feel through the eyes of God that all humans are the objects of his love regardless of their background and beliefs and that the whole world is God's wonderful creation.

Peter emphasized that believers who possess these qualities in increasing measure will not be found "ineffective and unproductive in knowledge of Christ." (2 Peter 1:8) Their calling and election will be sure. They will never fall. They "will receive a rich welcome into the eternal kingdom" of Christ. (2 Peter 1:10-11)

Peter realized as he was about to die that he needed to encourage the believers to wholesome thinking. He wrote: "I will always *remind* you of these things, even though you know them and are firmly established in the truth you now have. I think it is right to *refresh* your *memory*...I will make every effort to see that after my departure you will always be able to *remember* these things." (2 Peter 1:12-15)

What did Peter want them to remember? —the power of God's words!

The words of Christ

First, Peter reminded the believers that he spoke as a witness regarding the power and coming of Christ. Peter, James and John witnessed the transfiguration of Christ on the mountain. They heard the voice of the Majestic Glory, saying, "This is my Son, whom I love; with him I am well pleased." (Matthew 17:5)

Second, they knew that their experiences of Christ were predicted by the prophets from the Old Testament time. And that the prophesies about Christ "shine like light in a dark place until the day dawns and morning star rises in their hearts." (2 Peter 1:19)

Remembering and recalling God's words was the best antidote to the threat of destructive heresies that faced the early believers.

Peter sternly warned them, just as Christ also had forewarned his disciples (Matthew 7:15) that their worst enemies may be among themselves. (2 Peter 2:1) False teachers among the believers and false prophets among the people would be present who would secretly introduce destructive heresies. Peter described them as people who once were believers but now had turned from their sovereign Lord to teach and act contrary to the gospel. They had returned to their old ways, were exploitative, and were slanderous of celestial beings. They blasphemed. They caroused in open daylight. They reveled in their pleasure while they feasted with the believers. They were adulterous and seducers of the unstable. They used empty, boastful words and appealed to the lustful nature of those who believed. Worse, they promised freedom yet were depraved. (2 Peter 2:1-3) In short, they had stumbled in their faith and returned to the old ways of unrighteousness, abused their freedom in Christ, and turned their backs on the sacred commandments. False teachers should be recognized for who they were and avoided.

Words of the Prophets

Then there were scoffers who mocked the words of Christ regarding his second coming. "Where is this 'coming' since the world has gone on as it has since the creation?" (2 Peter 3:4) Peter reminded them that it was through God's words that the heaven existed and the earth was formed out of the water and by water. (Genesis 1:6, 8; 9-10) And by the word of God, the sinful world once was deluged and destroyed by water during Noah's time. (Genesis 6:5-7, 17) In like manner, in the future, also by God's word, the ungodly will be judged and destroyed, this time around, by fire. (2 Peter 3:10)

Some interpreted the Lord's slowness in coming as God not keeping his promise. They forgot that God's sense of time is unlike a human's concept of time. With the Lord, a day is like a thousand years, and a thousand years a day. (2 Peter 3:8) They do not understand God's patience and mercy in that God does not want anyone to perish, but wants *everyone* to come to repentance. (2 Peter 3:9) Extending this reasoning, waiting for two centuries for even one soul to be saved may be worth God's waiting. And when the Lord comes, the timing of his appearance will be like a thief—unexpected. On that day, the heavens will disappear with a roar; and the world will be destroyed by fire. (2 Peter 3:10)

Knowing this, that everything will be destroyed in this way, what kind of people ought we to be and how should we live?

5. *Live holy and godly lives.* (2 Peter 3:11) Look forward to a new heaven and a new earth where righteousness reigns. Realize that the Lord's patience means salvation. "Make every effort to be found spotless, blameless, and at peace with God" (2 Peter 3:14) and to stand fast in the faith and "grow in the grace and knowledge of our Lord and Savior Jesus Christ." (2 Peter 3:18)

Conclusion

The "eyes of the heart" of Peter see spirituality as a total transformation of the mind of the believer through a process of cognitive restructuring he called "wholesome thinking." Individually, it involves a change in the personality of the believer in terms of thinking, emotions and actions in order to conform to the characters of God. Collectively, believers become God's instruments of righteousness. The transformation was anchored on the words of the prophets and the words of Christ as told by the apostles. It suggested that the maturing spiritual growth of a person follows a trajectory of growth akin to biological development. We can see that the direction of the forces of change are centrifugal: first, transformation is at the core of one's being and identity when one is called to be a child of God; second, a process of purification and sanctification of the value system takes place to conform to God's standard of holiness; third, each individual believer is linked to each other to form the spiritual body of God and the church; and finally, the people of God, collectively exert positive changes in the world.

KEY POINTS:

- Peter wrote the two epistles to stimulate Christians to wholesome thinking.

- Obtainment of wholesome thinking relies on one constantly reflecting on the words of God and a cognitive restructuring of the mind to conform to God's ways of thinking. It leads to a change in personality that reflects God's nature.

- The central message that drives both epistles is that God empowers believers in Christ to become "a chosen people, a royal priesthood, a holy nation, a people belonging to God."

- The enduring words of the disciples point to a new birth into a living hope in Christ that prepares the mind for action.

- The action plan for the new mind called for believers to live a good life, as free men and as servants of God, in harmony, for the will of God, and a holy and godly life.

- The power of change emanates like a centrifugal force that starts within the individual, and all believers become a collective force of positive influence in the world.

- The paradigm of Christian spiritual growth starts with faith and reaches its pinnacle with love for all people.

- The second coming of Christ will be unexpected. God's timing is different from human's. God's patience is reflected in his desire that all men will be saved.

- Suffering for Christians takes on a new meaning: God allows it for the spiritual edification of the believers.

4. James: Authentic Life

SIGNIFICANCE:

Seek integration of faith and action. It is the sign of an authentic spiritual life.

James

"As the body without the spirit is dead, so faith without deeds is dead." (James 2:26)

Introduction

James, who was Jesus' half-brother, was presumed to be the author of this letter.[1] The letter was written probably around AD 52, after the Council of Jerusalem and after Paul's gospel was preached to the Jewish Diaspora and gentiles.[2] Growing up with Christ, James' contact with him was probably more intimate than what the other apostles could have had. However, he initially did not believe in the person of Christ and in his mission. He doubted the motives of Christ. When Jesus purposely stayed away from Judea because the Jews were waiting to kill him, James and his brothers were urging him to return to Judea. They thought Jesus had earthly political ambition. (John 7:2-5) Like people in one's hometown who do not understand and welcome their own prophets, James initially had difficulty accepting his brother as the Christ, the Messiah he claimed to be. But Christ appeared to him after his resurrection. (1 Corinthians 15:7) Later, St. Paul regarded James, along with Peter and John, as "pillars" of the early church. (Galatians 2:9) In between the period of Christ's appearance to him and his becoming a "pillar" of the early Jerusalem church, James underwent a spiritual transformation. We have no information on what transpired. But James became a highly regarded person and assumed a key position in the early church. He was a leader at the Council of Jerusalem that forged a compromise between the Jewish and Gentile Christians regarding the observance of Jewish rituals, particularly those dealing with circumcision and he wrote the decree in a letter delivered by Judas and Silas, with Paul and Barnabas, to the gentile Christians at Antioch. (Acts 15:13-29)

The transformation of James' perception and belief in Jesus is significant. It is not hard to surmise that because of the transparency of Christ's life to James, he must have had a particular insight into the teachings of Christ and the life he lived. In fact, James' thinking as reflected in his writings, particularly on topics related to Christ's Sermon on the Mount, revealed many similarities.[3]

Both James and Jesus spoke Aramaic, the Jewish language of their time. James also had knowledge of Greek. He was a strong adherent of the Jewish traditions. He was familiar with the Jewish wisdom literature such as the proverbs, and parables and the sage advice concerning the conduct of every day life.[4] After the impact of Paul's gospel was felt among the gentile believers in which some had considered Paul's position on the observance of the Mosaic laws to be optional, there were evolving misinterpretations of the role of *faith* and *works*. Some had thought one could ignore behavior as long as one had faith. Although both James and Paul held the same positions regarding the doctrine of *justification by faith in Christ;* the difference was one of emphasis. Paul emphasized the inner transformation; James stressed the importance of living one's faith through deeds. One is justified through faith not works, but it doesn't mean deeds do not grow out of faith. James was concerned that some believers had misinterpreted that *justification by faith in Christ* to mean a de-emphasis of works or deeds, as though faith could be dissociated from works. James sought to correct this misinterpretation and that was the main motivation for his letter.[5] He also was vitally interested in how the gospel could be accepted by the Jewish believers without them having to forsake the Mosaic traditions and rituals. James wanted all believers, Jews and gentiles, to understand that the revelatory wisdom of Christ does not mean forsaking all their traditions. He was not anti-Pauline in his position. He wanted to clarify what true faith was. To James, faith, the foundation of salvation and spirituality, is not merely an intellectual percept or concept, it must be anchored in action. True faith cannot be separated from action. This is the central message of his letter to the twelve Jewish tribes scattered in many nations. And James explicated this message in a straight-forward and convincing manner. James emphasized paying attention to the practical aspects of living— speech, attitude, boasting, and patience during suffering— to buttress his argument that faith and deeds are inseparable.

James

To James, the authenticity of a Christian faith was tested in trials that refined and brought out the core of one's inner spiritual "self" and was constantly manifested in one's behavior. In other words, he emphasized living a life that was *integrated* spiritually, morally, emotionally, and behaviorally—a faith that was alive in action.

But first, James wanted believers to understand the distinction between two kinds of testing of one's faith: spiritual versus carnal or earthly. Spiritual testing is *trial of faith*; the carnal or earthly one is *temptation*. The two phenomena differ in the origin of the impulse, in its development, and in its consequences. (Figure 2) Trial of faith was regarded by James as part of the spiritual maturational process of a Christian life. Once born-again through the acceptance of the word of God and the indwelling of the Holy Spirit, the spiritual life of a believer, like that of a newborn baby, must grow and reach maturity. And in the maturational process, trials are inevitable as they refine the development of that faith to make it "complete, wanting in nothing." It is this deep realization, conviction and hope that enable Christians to regard their "trials" with "pure joy." As Peter had aptly described it, the testing of faith is like the purification of gold into its purest form. (1 Peter 1:7). He added, "Who is going to harm you if you are eager to do good? But even if you should suffer for what is right, you are blessed." (1 Peter 3:13) Christ said that those who are persecuted because of righteousness are blessed because the kingdom of heaven will be theirs. (Matthew 5:10-11)

The reframing of the trial of faith from suffering to joy may not be easy to comprehend. It is not a rationalization. Rather, it is borne out of a deep realization and conviction that God has willed and permitted such experiences to happen to his people. The meaning of suffering is linked to a higher order, to God's will and for the edification of the self. As in the trials of Job, the calamities that befell Job seemed puzzling to him and his friends at first. For example, Eliphaz, Job's friend considered his suffering a result of sin. (Job 4:7-8) While Job was undergoing the trials of his faith, his experiences were extremely painful. With God's permission, the devil stripped away every layer of Job's human comfort—his reputation, position, assets, children and family, and even his health—to lay bare Job's spirituality and see whether Job was going to falter and abandon his faith. But Job persevered. The outcome of his trials of faith revealed the authenticity of his spirituality. His actions and words did not deny God. In the end, God doubled Job's blessings. Thus, the trial of faith is a purifying process to bring out an authentic spiritual life, and the best of one's character. It must be understood from God's perspective to enable one to persevere while in pain and distress. And the ultimate reward is a "crown of life that God has promised to those who love him." (James 1:12)

On the other hand, the testing of temptation assumes a different nature and perspective. One is tempted because of the enticements of the desires of the "flesh"—instinct, impulses and biologic needs that although in themselves are not sinful and wrong, but when acted out in a manner contrary to God's precepts and will, could corrupt one's moral fiber, injure others, and ultimately lead to sin and death.

King David's sin is the quintessential example. Enticed by his sexual desire for the beautiful Bathsheba, the king summoned her to his court and had intercourse with her. When he found out that Bathsheba was pregnant, he plotted to cover up his sin. Eventually, he had Uriah, Bathsheba's husband, killed in battle. David suffered greatly for his transgression. His faith in God and his spirituality were tested. But this kind of testing stemmed from his succumbing to the temptation of the flesh. Its origin is not from God but from the "devil." He was enticed by what he saw, his sexual desire, and he used flawed judgment and suffered for his sins.

Kinds of trial	Spiritual	Carnal
Origin	God, spiritual	Devil, of the flesh
Development	Spiritual maturation	Enticements of desires
Consequences	Spiritual growth	Sins, death

Figure 2. Two kinds of trials

Trials of faith in daily life

Having explicated the two kinds of trials, James went on to address some basic and practical aspects of living: control of the tongue, discrimination, matching faith with deeds or actions, boasting about future plans, and patience during suffering. Should the trials of one's faith include these practical daily experiences? James seemed to imply that they certainly do. His discussions of these aspects of practical living were interspersed with his exposition of the unity of faith and deeds.

I believe how one handles the mundane aspects of daily living strongly reveal one's faith and spirituality. True, calamities and pain test the real fiber of one's faith and spirituality. But to prevail in one's daily struggles against certain attitudinal, emotional and behavioral challenges that may lead to depression, anxiety, desperation, stress and pain that drag one away from God's precepts and way of life, these too are trials. Often, it is these mundane challenges that test the veracity of one's beliefs and reveal the authenticity of one's spirituality and character. In this sense, let us consider what James had to say:

1. Taming our tongue
"Everyone should be quick to listen, slow to speak, and slow to become angry." (James 1:19) What wise advice that is, and will most definitely help to promote harmonious interpersonal relationships! As a psychiatrist who is trained to listen, I resonate with what James said. The distortion of perception, of attributing wrong

motives to others, and other misunderstandings occur as often as they do because one does not listen, and listen well. Before one speaks and gets angry, one should listen carefully. Without clearly discerning what the other person is saying, and jumping to conclusions and then speaking out in anger, the tongue can provoke arguments and cause irreparable harm.

The tongue, as James pointed out, is a powerful instrument. What one says reveals the true nature of one's being—carnal or spiritual. The tongue can boast or show humility; corrupt or build up or even get one into serious trouble setting "the whole course of his life on fire." (James 3:6) The tongue is capable of utmost deceit and contradiction, of both praising and cursing. How could one tame one's tongue so that it becomes an organ of blessings to oneself and others? How can one prevent the paradox and confusion, as James aptly described it, that the same tongue praises God and curses men as if both "fresh water" and "salt water" could flow from the same spring? The critical factor in the taming of the tongue as James explained it is to anchor one's faith on the words of God. Use God's words as a spiritual mirror. The propensity to blurt out words that come from one's sinful nature and self— utterance of what James called "moral filth and the evil"— must be put aside. In its place, James wanted the believers to take to heart what the word of God teaches. Believers can use the words of God to introspect before they speak and act. The words of God act as spiritual mirrors to lead them to an understanding of the true state of affairs. The spirit of God instructs, encourages and convinces. It enhances that inner voice of conscience that must not be stifled or silenced. James implored believers to use them to enhance spirituality. Keep a tight rein on one's tongue. Think through what one wants to say in light of one's understanding of God's word. And be careful not to become angry. Overcoming the tendency of the tongue to say negative things is a trial of faith. It is the first step of "keeping oneself from being polluted by the world." (James 1:27) It is the royal road to true spirituality. "If anyone considers himself religious and yet does not keep a tight rein on his tongue, he deceives himself and his religion is worthless." (James 1:26) James wanted believers to know that he who controls his tongue shows deep spirituality. True spirituality starts with controlling one's tongue.

2. *Show your wisdom and understanding by one's good life, and by deeds done in humility.*

Just as there are two types of trials, there are two kinds of wisdom: earthly and heavenly. James's admonition to control the tongue is an example of the manifestation of a wisdom that "comes from heaven." It is the acting out of a spirituality that is anchored on the words of God. It is done in humility. And it is a manifestation of an inner transformation of one's character that conforms to what Peter describes as the "divine nature." (2 Peter 1:4) It is what the "eyes of the heart" of James saw. James described the wisdom that comes from heaven: *pure, peace-loving, considerate, submissive, full of mercy and good fruits, impartial and sincere.* (James 3:17)

James urged believers to purify their faith from earthly, unspiritual "wisdom" that comes from the devil—carnal knowledge that is meant to corrupt and exploit others, and is a manifestation of envy and selfish ambitions. Where these exist, one finds disorder and evil practices.

But how does one obtain wisdom from above? James admonishes believers to ask God through unwavering prayer and to ask for the right reason. James asserted that if one prayed for wisdom for the furtherance of God's will, for the edification of others, and not for the fulfillment of one's pleasures, God *would* answer every prayer.

If any of you lacks wisdom, he should ask God, who gives generously to all without finding fault, and it will be given to him. But when he asks he must believe and not doubt, because he who doubts is like a wave of the sea, blown and tossed by the wind. That man should not think he will receive anything from the Lord; he is a double-minded man, unstable in all he does. (James 1:5-8)

You do not have, because you do not ask God. When you ask, you do not receive, because you ask with the wrong motives, that you may spend what you get on your pleasures. (James 4:2-3)

Christ said, "Ask and it shall be given to you." (Matthew 7:7)

To be wise and understanding, to be able to show wisdom in one's life, to speak in ways that are pleasing to God and acceptable to men and in a spirit of humility, one needs to ask God for wisdom that "comes from heaven", with unwavering faith and with the right motives.

3. Do what the word says

"Religion that God our Father accepts as pure and faultless is this: to look after orphans and widows in their distress and to keep oneself from being polluted by the world." (James 1:27) James encouraged believers to rein in their tongue as a way to keep oneself pure. The other aspect of true spirituality was doing what God's words say. Keeping oneself pure and free from being polluted by the world and caring for orphans and widows in their distress are two aspects of the same phenomena—the yin/yang of spirituality. Christ said in his Sermon on the Mount, "Blessed are the pure in heart, for they will *see* God." (Matthew 5:8) The brother of Christ defined for believers what true religion and spirituality are: keeping oneself morally pure and caring for the downtrodden and less fortunate. One can easily be deceived and deceive oneself when overcome by the rush of "compassionate" feelings for others. But without actions those feelings mean nothing. Passion without action is dead. Here I'm reminded of the picture of a rich Russian aristocrat who was moved to tears when seeing scenes of suffering in an opera. After the show, she stoically sped off in a horse-drawn carriage on the snow-covered roads amidst a throng of homeless people, all stretching their arms out, begging. We need to convert our passion into action. Christ, in the story of the Samaritan, showed believers what true faith and compassion are. The trial of faith requires the acting out of one's compassion to look after the less fortunate. It is that philan-thropic attitude that makes the world go merrily around. It reflects true spirituality when one acts on impulses of love. It's what this one bumper sticker says: "commit random acts of kindness." The scripture is clear on what God's value is: he chose and preferred the poor and the humble in spirit to inherit his kingdom. "Blessed are the poor in spirit, for theirs is the kingdom of heaven...Blessed are the meek, for they will inherit the earth." (Matthew 5:3,5) In Handel's Messiah we hear the words, "Every valley shall be exalted and every mountain made low." James challenged anyone's claim to spirituality without action: "Show me your faith without deeds, and I will show you my faith by what I do." (James 2:18) Christ's brother witnessed the authenticity of Christ's spirituality and wanted believers to emulate Christ's behavior and live his teachings. Paul beautifully explained it:

> But what does it (*the righteousness that is by faith*) say? "The word is near you; it is in your mouth and in your heart," that is, the word of faith we are proclaiming: that if you confess with your mouth, "Jesus is Lord," and believe in your heart that God raised him from the dead, you will be saved. For it is with your heart that you believe and are justified, and it is with your mouth that you confess and are saved. (Romans 10: 8-10)

Paul could have just said believe in your heart and you will be saved. Why confession? Because believing is an inner phenomenon and confession affirms what one believes. The distance between the heart and the tongue may be short, but to be able to say and truly act what one's heart believes, that process must traverse a path of an inner transformation of character that is the work of the Holy Spirit. Just as faith without action is dead, the tongue must say what the heart *believes and sees* in order to be saved. The unity of faith and action proves an authentic spiritual life.

4. *Do not discriminate*
Discrimination is the antithesis of spirituality. It smacks of hypocrisy. It is the stumbling block that frequently causes many unbelievers to turn away from the true faith. It is contrary to God's

supreme law of love. James' admonition was clear: don't show favoritism.

Discrimination stems from an attitude of judging people according to their outer appearances. But its sinister manifestation is a "put down" attitude and a behavioral statement that says, "You're not good enough; you're smaller, less than, or insignificant." It defies and acts contrary to the basic tenet of God's law, "Love thy neighbor as yourself."

James used the example of how one tends to show favoritism toward the rich, the outwardly adorned and the beautiful to illustrate his point. Two men come to a meeting, one is rich wearing a gold ring and fine clothes, and the other is poor and dressed in shabby clothes. The good seat is given to the rich and the poor is allowed to stand or sit in a bad location. Isn't that discrimination and doesn't that reflect evil thoughts? James admonished believers not to show favoritism, for God does not. In fact, "God has chosen those who are poor in the eyes of the world to be rich in faith and to inherit the kingdom he promised those who love him." (James 2:5) The first beatitude says: "Blessed are the poor in spirit, for theirs is the kingdom of heaven." (Matthew 5:3)

If one is spiritual, love is in one's heart. Love will guide believers to the right action: to be sensitive to other's feelings, and to treat everybody with respect and equality. James asked them to "Speak and act as those who are going to be judged by the law that gives freedom." (James 2:12). In the final analysis of God's value system, "mercy triumphs over judgment." (James 2:13)

5. *Faith and deeds*

Consistent with the themes explored above, James summed up his cardinal view of the true nature of faith: actions. "If a man claims to have faith but has no deeds? Can such faith save him?..faith by itself, if it is not accompanied by action, is dead." (James 2: 14, 17).

The inseparable unity of faith and action is the reflection of true spirituality. One's beliefs have to be constantly tested for their veracity. It is easy to rationalize into thinking one has love when in fact one's behavior speaks to the contrary. Any religion that teaches one to kill is a false religion, for it does not uphold the sanctity of life and debases fellow human beings. Aggression committed in the name of God is hypocrisy and sinful. It does not change human hearts. It only leads to destruction and death.

James wanted to emphasize this point. Christians can be lulled by the message of love and become "callous" in their behavior and begin to restrain their impulses to help. It is like experiencing love burn-out. Yet, without action, words of love mean nothing. If one wishes a hungry brother well, to keep warm and well fed, but withholds the giving of food or clothes, what good is one's wishes and prayers? True faith is buttressed by action.

A Christian's message of "justification by faith" does not reside in the intellect alone. It is not enough to utter words that do not reflect a true change of character. The apostles emphasized that faith is manifested through actions, and James said it clearly. Abraham's faith is shown by his leaving his homeland when he was told by God to go to a foreign country. He carried out God's instruction to sacrifice his son Isaac right up until the very last minute before God stopped him. And even Rahab the prostitute who played a key role in assisting Joshua and the Israelites in the conquest of Jericho, believed the words of the oath of the Israeli spies to help her and her family and that they would be spared death. She put her life in danger when she hid the spies, helped them escape to the hills, and tied the scarlet cord on her window as a sign of identification as she summoned all members of her family to her home. Her faith in the words of the Israeli spies, matched by her actions, saved her and her entire family when Joshua and his men attacked Jericho.

6. *Boasting about tomorrow*

What's wrong if one plans for a business trip in the future? Is it inherently wrong to earn money and to say so openly? Not so, unless one boasts and becomes arrogant.

One plans on the assumption that tomorrow will come. One sets priorities based on the premise that one's breath will last and one's heart will keep ticking. But there are those who boast and brag as though they are in control of their destiny. James wanted believers to see things in a different perspective: life belongs to God; humans are mere guardians of his trust and of their bodies. The capacity to act on the future is predicated on the constancy of things, space and time. I live in an earthquake-prone city, San Francisco. Most San Franciscans are resigned to the thought that earthquakes are inevitable. But our faith that an earthquake will most likely not hit tomorrow keeps our lives humming along. But we would be foolish if we didn't make preparations for disasters, though we cannot control their happening. In the same light, James wanted believers to understand their priorities: it's life and that they should put their trust in God, the author of life. James reminded believers that life is transient, like a fleeting mist. Although one plans for the future, one should do so in humility. The saying, "If it is the Lord's will, we will live and do this and that." is not just a cliché, it reflects true faith and spirituality that acknowledges that one's life is fleeting, that it belongs to God. Just like a belief that one will survive an earthquake, one merely lives by faith when one assumes that one's breath will sustain her or him into the future. Coming to grips with this fact and acting accordingly is wisdom from above. And if one truly believes this tenet, one will take care of one's body in a new spiritual perspective. Believers will be acting out of a sense of grace. They will not boast or brag about themselves and their accomplishments. They will be living on a higher ethical plain. James said, "Anyone, then, who knows the good he ought to do and doesn't, sins." (James 4:17) Faith compels ethical action in humility.

7. Warning to the rich oppressors

The rich are enjoined by James to be humble, fair, to live uprightly, and to shun evil. They should not exploit the poor. In God's scale of things, the rich and the poor share the same life breath; God makes sunshine and brings rain for both the rich and the poor. That equality in spirit has been stressed by both Peter and Paul. "Submit to one another out of reverence for Christ." (Ephesians 5:21) Slaves and masters, wives and husbands, children and parents are to relate in a manner that reflects equality, mutuality, respect and love. True faith does not exploit, demean or harm others. On the contrary, it uplifts and builds up others. There is a willingness to share one's wealth with the less fortunate.

8. Patience in suffering

James returned to this theme of the *trial of faith* as he exhorted the Jewish believers to "Be patient, then, brothers, until the Lord's coming." (James 5:7) He shows his faith in the Messiah, the resurrected Christ. Suffering while waiting for the Lord's coming is bearable and is to be welcomed, just as the farmer waits for the land to yield its crop and is patient for both the autumn and the spring rain. In the first chapter, he reminded the believers that the trial of faith develops perseverance and perseverance must finish its work so that believers may be mature and complete. "Be patient and stand firm, because the Lord's coming is near." (James 5:8) This message once more reminds believers that God's timing is unlike ours. God is patient with us, not wanting anyone to perish, but everyone to come to repentance. (2 Peter 3:8-9)

True faith has a heavenly perspective that empowers and sustains a believer in the midst of earthly suffering. It can turn pain into joy, even pure joy.

Conclusion

James, Christ's brother, revealed his spirituality as he expounded on the unity of faith and deeds. The eyes of his heart saw faith and action as the inseparable cornerstone that anchors one's life. He expressed his faith in action by showing it in the practical matters of daily life: In speech, in attitude, in behavior, in giving, in prayers, and in suffering. A believer in Christ shows his or her faith and spirituality by living them.

KEY POINTS:

- James wrote this epistle to correct misconceptions about faith and works. Faith and work are unified. Faith without work or deeds is dead.

- There are two kinds of "testing" of one's faith: the spiritual and the carnal that differ in the origins of their impulse, in their development and in their consequences.

- There are two kinds of "wisdom": the heavenly and the earthly.

- The wisdom that comes from heaven is pure, peace-loving, considerate, submissive, full of mercy and good fruits, impartial and sincere.

- True faith and spirituality are manifested in the activities of daily life: in speech, attitude, giving, and in perseverance in pain and suffering.

- The control of one's tongue is the royal road to spirituality.

- Do not discriminate. Discrimination is the antithesis of spirituality and is against the basic tenet of the law of God—love.

- Boasting about future plans is arrogant because this attitude reflects a belief that one is in total control of one's life which one is not.

- Perseverance while waiting for the Lord's coming reaps joy even though it may bring temporary suffering.

SECTION 2:

THE CHALLENGES OF SPIRITUALITY

5. King Saul: Self-Esteem

SIGNIFICANCE:

Build self-esteem. It is the basis of feeling good, the foundation of strong relationships, and the bedrock of a steady spirituality.

King Saul

"You were once small in your own eyes" (1 Samuel 15:17)

Introduction

Saul appeared at a pivotal moment in Israel's history. Tall, young, handsome, ambitious, a warrior and personally chosen and anointed first King of Israel by the powerful Prophet Samuel to lead his nascent nation, he seemed the right person for the job, at the right time. God helped him win his first decisive battle against the Ammonites. Saul had David, one of Israel's greatest warriors as a commander of his army, his personal armor-bearer, captain of his bodyguard, son-in-law, and personal musician. Saul's future seemed so full of promise. Yet, the end of his life in contrast to his glorious beginning was quite pathetic. Deserted by God with no prophet to turn to for advice, he approached a witch at Endor to summon the spirit of Samuel, only to be rebuked by Samuel's spirit and foretold of his death and the defeat of his army at the hands of the Philistines. In his final battle against the Philistines, his sons were killed, his army was defeated, and Saul, himself was critically wounded. He ended his life by plunging his sword into his body.

Why?

Background

Some time between 1050-1010 B.C., the elders of Israel, fearful of their surrounding enemies and having no confidence in Samuel's corrupt sons to succeed him as judges,[1] which were all that ruled Israel at that time, asked Samuel to choose a king, "now appoint a king to lead us, such as all the other nations have." (1 Samuel 8:4-5)

Although this displeased Samuel and God, God gave in to their request. This marked Israel's transition from a theocratic state to a monarchy. Saul was chosen and anointed King by Samuel.

Even though a king ruled over Israel, God's covenant with Israel and the new king remained in effect: fear the Lord, serve and obey him and do not rebel against his commandments or you will suffer God's rejection. (1 Samuel 12:14-15)

Saul

Saul was reportedly thirty years old when he became king. (1 Samuel 13:1) He was a head taller than other Israelites. Despite his impressive physical stature, there were early hints that a feeling of "smallness" pervaded his character. When told by Samuel that he would be anointed king, he asked, "But am I not a Benjamite, from the *smallest* tribe of Israel, and is not my clan, the *least* of all the clans of the tribe of Benjamin?" When Samuel assembled the people of Israel to declare the selection of Saul and present him as king, Saul was nowhere to be found. Saul "hid himself among the baggage." (1 Samuel 10:22) Although he was physically impressive, his behavior, demeanor and self-perception suggested otherwise.

Two early incidents in his life tested his character and spirituality and served to reveal his flaws.

The first incidence was how he responded to Samuel's instructions before the battle with the Philistines. Samuel had told Saul to wait for him for seven days before embarking on the battle. When Samuel did not arrive at the appointed time on the seventh day, Saul took it upon himself to perform the priestly function of making the burnt offering. Just as he finished making the offering, Samuel arrived. Samuel confronted Saul with his disobedience to the Lord's commands and told him that the consequences of his behavior would be that his kingdom would not endure and that the Lord had sought out another person to succeed him. (1 Samuel 13:13-14)

The episode revealed a fault-line in Saul's character: insecurity, self-centeredness, a tendency on his part to put his personal needs and agenda ahead of both God's will and of his people's needs. He had panicked and in that panic, due to the stress, he made calamitous mistakes.

In the ensuing battle with the Philistines, even though the Israelites were out-numbered, God was still there with Israel. Saul's son, Jonathan and his armor-bearer infiltrated the Philistine's outpost and killed twenty Philistines. Then God sent a panic through the whole Philistine army. On that day, Israel routed the Philistines.

But Saul now became keenly absorbed in pursuit of his own agenda and ignored the needs of his army. He issued an order and bound his people to an oath not to eat food before evening came, so that he could have time to avenge himself on his enemies. This prohibition greatly distressed his army. They were tired and hungry, the men felt faint from the long fight. Returning from the front-line, Jonathan was unaware of the oath, and ate some honey. When Saul found out that Jonathan had violated the oath, he maintained that Jonathan must die. The people, though, were not willing to go along with this. They asked: Death to Jonathan, his son, the hero that saved the day for Israel? The people knew better. "Not a hair of his head will fall to the ground." (1 Samuel 14:45) The intervention of the people saved Jonathan. But Saul lost prestige. As commander-in-chief, his judgment had been called into question.

The second test, which was much more serious and egregious, blatantly displayed the deep fissures in Saul's character. Samuel instructed Saul to carry out God's command to completely annihilate the Amalekites—no person or animal was to be spared—as a punishment for waylaying the Israelites when they came up from Egypt. Yet, "Saul and the army spared Agag, king of Amalekites and the best of the sheep and cattle, the fat calves and lambs—everything that was good." (1 Samuel 15:9) After defeating the Amalekites, he went to Carmel to build a monument in his own honor. (1 Samuel 15:12)

When Samuel approached Saul, Saul reported that he had carried out the Lord's instructions. Yet, he rationalized the keeping of the booty of livestock by shifting his responsibility to his soldiers, saying, "The soldiers brought them from the Amalekites; they spared the best of the sheep and cattle to sacrifice to the Lord *your* God." (1 Samuel 15:15) Through Samuel's persistent and penetrating questions, Saul finally admitted that he had sinned by violating God's command and Samuel's instructions. In his admittance of guilt, Saul confessed to a revealing fact about himself, "...I was afraid of the people and so I gave in to them." The King was afraid of his own people? When it pertained to matters related to his personal agenda, as in issuing an order to his soldiers not to eat food until his personal vendetta was fulfilled, he pursued his foolish order with single mindedness. Yet when he needed to adhere to God's commands and knowing that those commands had far-reaching implications for him, his kingdom and his people, Saul was careless, callous and indecisive. He let his fear of his people influence him and blatantly ignored Samuel's clear warning of the covenant and the condition that had established the monarchy and his kingship in the first place. He overstepped the boundary and abused his power.

Samuel's confrontation with Saul revealed an aspect of Saul's character that underlaid his simultaneous feelings of insecurity and self-importance. Samuel said to him, "Although you were once *small* in your own eyes, did you not become the head of the tribes of Israel?" (1 Samuel 15:17) Samuel saw that Saul perceived himself as psychologically "small." At a deeper emotional level, Saul's emotional "size" was inconsistent with his physical stature. Although he was the king, supposedly the most powerful and "biggest" man in Israel at the time, his actions did not exude majestic confidence and correctness of judgments. His low self-esteem[2] contributed to his making foolish mistakes which ultimately led to God's rejection of his kingship. Samuel pronounced:

Because you have rejected the word of the Lord,
He has rejected you as king. (1 Samuel 15:23)

The Lord has torn the kingdom of Israel from you today and has given it to one of your neighbors—to one better than you. (1 Samuel 15:28)

Saul knew that his days as king were numbered. He must have wondered who that person "better" than he was and who would succeed him. And this must have intensified his already deep sense of insecurity and anxiety.

In addition to his feeling of "smallness", Saul experienced bouts of emotional episode wherein "an evil spirit from the Lord tormented him." (1 Samuel 16:14) It was Saul's emotional instability that prompted his attendants to suggest bringing David to play the harp to soothe Saul's tormented feelings.

His emotional state early on showed that he suffered from mood swings. Saul's moods would vacillate between episodes of emotional turmoil that required soothing music to relieve his distress to periods of angry outbursts and, later, murderous impulses. Several occurrences of his mood disturbance were preceded by David's military success. It seems that David's success only accentuated his feelings of inferiority and "smallness" and that may have been one of the triggers for his mood disturbance.

The interaction between Saul and David further reveals Saul's character defects.

David

David was brought into Saul's court to play the harp to soothe Saul's emotional distress. Saul took an immediate liking to David—young, fine-looking, ruddy, articulate, a brave man, a warrior and a talented harpist. Moreover, the "Lord was with him." Saul made him one of his armor-bearers.

David's heroic triumph over Goliath greatly enhanced his standing among his people. And Saul was a first-hand witness to David's courage, determination, prowess and reliance on the Lord, character traits quite opposite to Saul's.

At the height of his success, when throngs of women were greeting King Saul and cheering David and his men as they were returning from a victorious battle against the Philistines, Saul felt bitter and angered by the refrain of the women's choruses:

> Saul has slain his thousands,
> and David his tens of thousands. (1 Samuel 18:7)

The comparison was too much for Saul to take. "They have credited David with tens of thousands," he thought, "but me with only thousands. What more can he get but the kingdom?" (1 Samuel 18:8)

The refrain of the women must have sent a shockwave that shattered Saul's fragile self-esteem. Suddenly, he realized that here was a man, acknowledged by the crowd to be "bigger" and "stronger" than he was and that could be a potential competitor for his throne. The stark, public comparison between him and David was a deep humiliation. His first thought was: "What more can he get but the kingdom?" He was seized by jealousy and became fearful of David. In his mind, David became an immediate threat to his well-being and his kingship. It did not matter whether God had a hand in delivering the military victory to him that day. He suddenly realized that in all Israel, David must be *the* person predicted by Samuel who was "better" than he was to succeed him. To save his kingship, David had to be removed and destroyed. Saul's insecurity spewed forth poisonous clouds of jealousy and hatred that eventually erupted into intense murderous impulses toward the very person that earlier had brought him such a decisive victory, emotional comfort and honor. Almost in an instant, David, the loyal warrior, became David, the potential usurper of the throne. "And from that time on Saul kept a jealous eye on David." (1 Samuel 18:9)

The very next day, Saul lapsed into an intense emotional state described this way: an "evil spirit from God came forcefully upon him." He was raving in his house and while David was playing the harp to soothe him, Saul hurled his spear at David to pin him against the wall. Although David was able to elude him twice, Saul's attempts to murder David started a personal vendetta and campaign to eliminate David. Subsequently, Saul would leave no stone unturned, no patch of ground untraversed, simply to hunt down his perceived adversary like "looking for a flea—as one hunts partridge in the mountain."(1 Samuel 26:20) David became Saul's mortal enemy.

Saul's fear of David didn't diminish but intensified. First, he plotted to have David killed at the hands of the Philistines by asking David to deliver 100 Philistine foreskins as the price for his daughter Michal in marriage. When this failed, and he realized "that the Lord was with David and that his daughter Michal loved David, Saul became still more afraid of him, and he remained his enemy the rest of his days." (1 Samuel 18:28-29)

Then Saul ordered David killed. Saul attempted to ensnare David was during a New Moon festival in which David was expected to dine with him. But with Jonathan's help, David hid. When Saul discovered that Jonathan had sided with David, shielding him from the king's trap, Saul's temper erupted against Jonathan. He cursed his son, ordered him to bring David to him. And when Jonathan questioned him as to the reasons why he wanted to kill David, Saul hurled his spear at his own son. (1 Samuel 20:32-33) In his fury, Saul revealed the reason of his fear of David. "As long as the son of Jesse lives on this earth, neither you nor your kingdom will be established." (1 Samuel 20:31)

Whatever glimpse of insight Saul might have had into his own behavior, it was short-lived. Jonathan initially was able to convince his father to spare David, citing as evidence how David had risked his life when he fought against Goliath and brought Saul a great victory. "David had done no wrong and that there was no reason to kill an innocent man" Jonathan implored. Saul initially listened and even took an oath not to kill David. (1 Samuel 19:6) But when another war broke out and David again triumphed against the Philistines, Saul returned to his old hateful self. He lapsed into another emotional spell, and again, tried to kill David with his spear. This time, David escaped for good.

He fled to the Adullam cave where about four hundred men joined him. Then David and his men escaped to the forest of Hereth. Although David showed no intention of attacking Saul, the fact that David now had a small band of fighting men must have further aggravated Saul's feeling of insecurity. He began to grossly distort and misinterpret events and he became paranoid. At a gathering on the hill at Gibeah, while surrounded by all his officials, Saul falsely accused them of conspiring against him, not telling him that his son had made a covenant with David and that Jonathan had incited David "to lie in wait for him." (1 Samuel 22:8)

During his pursuit of David, Saul's head shepherd, Doeg, the Edomite who had witnessed David's visit with Ahimelech, the priest, reported to Saul what he had seen and heard; Saul sent for Ahimelech and his whole family of priests. He accused Ahimelech of conspiring against him and being an accomplice of David's. (1 Samuel 22:13) He ignored Ahimelech's plea of innocence of the whole affair between the king and David. Saul ordered Ahimelech and all the priests killed. On that day, Saul ordered all the inhabitants and animals of the town of Nob to perish as well. Saul's suspiciousness, lapse of judgment, insecurity, paranoia, anger and murderous impulses had spun completely out of control.

And he was relentless in his pursuit of David. Twice, David had a chance to avenge himself by killing Saul. Yet, David would never allow himself nor any one else to lay a hand on Saul, the Lord's anointed. In the first instance outside a cave in En Gedi, David asked Saul as to why he listened to the sinister advice of others who told him, "David is bent on harming you?" What had he done to deserve Saul's anger? David reminded him how he had spared Saul and did not return evil deeds with more evil deeds. He showed deep reverence towards God's anointed. He pleaded with Saul to consider his innocence. In response, Saul showed perhaps the rarest instance of tenderness towards David since David had fled from him when he said to David, "Is that your voice, David my son?" Saul wept. He acknowledged his fault and was moved by David's magnanimity in sparing his life. He told David he would be king some day and asked David to take an oath that David would not cut off his descendants or wipe out his name from his father's family.

But his admission of fault, like his insight, was short-lived. Later, when the Ziphites told Saul that David was hiding in the hills of Hakilah, Saul again went down to search for him. An opportunity came up again for David to kill Saul. But David again spared him. David pleaded with Saul to weigh the evidence he had against

David. He asked him: Was it God's incitement or the scheme of men? Why was the king of Israel pursuing him like a flea?

Saul again admitted his fault and to his foolish actions. He promised David not to harm him and invited David to return to his court. But David knew that Saul could not be trusted. They parted ways permanently.

Saul's suicide

The end of Saul's life was sad. The spirit of God had long left him. Samuel had died. He had caused David to flee. His prophets had all been killed. This left him with no one to consult with during his final battle against the Philistines. Desperate and forlorn, he secretly went to consult a witch of Endor to summon the spirit of Samuel, only to be rebuked and told by Samuel's spirit that he, his sons and his army would be handed over to the Philistines.

The Philistines fought hard against Israel. Saul's army ended up scattered with his three sons, including Jonathan, killed. Saul was critically wounded. To avoid the abuse and ignominy of being captured alive by his enemy, Saul took the only redeeming way out of a desperate situation. He plunged his sword into his body.

On learning of Saul and Jonathan's death, David lamented:

Your glory, O Israel, lies slain on your heights,
How the mighty have fallen! (2 Samuel 1:19)

Conclusion

Saul's life was complex and complicated due to the transitional nature of Israel at that time. His actions should be viewed in light of this historical moment and in the context of both his spiritual and psychological make-up. Being thrust into a new role, one that he did not choose, he had to rely solely on Samuel, who did not give him enough support. His relationships with both Samuel and David were ambivalent. Confronted by his internal emotional torment while the enemies were lining up against his nation, Saul constantly waged two battles at the same time: one external and the other internal.

From a spiritual viewpoint, Saul's actions must ultimately be seen and judged in light of the sovereign will of God as revealed in the covenant and how Saul exercised his free will in carrying out God's command. In this, he was tested and fell short.

The account in 1 Chronicles succinctly summarized the providential reason for Saul's death: "Saul died because he was unfaithful to the Lord; he did not keep the word of the Lord and even consulted a medium for guidance, and did not inquire of the Lord. So the Lord put him to death and turned his kingdom over to David son of Jesse." (1 Chronicles 10:13-14)

There are many spiritual lessons that could be gleaned from the life of Saul. The following verses in 1 Samuel speak for themselves:

- "Fear the Lord and serve and obey him and do not rebel against his commandments." (1 Samuel 12:14)
- "Be sure to fear the Lord and serve him faithfully with all your heart." (1 Samuel 12:24)
- "To obey is better than sacrifice, and to heed is better than the fat of rams." (1 Samuel 15:22)
- "Rebellion is like the sin of divination, and arrogance like the evil of idolatry." (1 Samuel 15:23)
- "Man looks at the outward appearance, but the Lord looks at the heart." (1 Samuel 16:7)

From a psychological perspective, one can discern that Saul suffered from a tormenting emotional condition, with prominent mood swings. Although there is not enough historical information that can confidently shed light on the nature of his emotional state, from a modern psychiatric perspective, "An evil spirit from God" could be a phenomenon of a dissociative identity disorder, a possession syndrome, depression, schizophrenia, or a bipolar (manic-depressive) disorder.[3] However, his mood swings strongly suggest a mood disturbance, possibly a bipolar disorder. If it turns out to be bipolar, knowing as we do now that bipolar disorder is a mental illness with a strong genetic predisposition, one can speculate on the possibility that a biological underpinning may have predisposed him to his mood disturbance.

But Saul's behavior, like all human behavior, cannot be explained on the basis of genetics and biology alone. Developmental and environmental factors often act to contribute to the stress that precipitates the onset of emotional disturbance. Samuel recognized Saul's emotional insufficiency when he told Saul that he was "once *small in his own eyes.*" Although he was physically taller than most Israelites, Saul's self-perception was that he really was quite "small." He lacked self-worth and/or self-esteem, giving rise to a feeling that something was lacking or defective in his psychological make-up. It seems that Saul's emotional growth and development had not kept pace with his physical growth. He may have been a thirty-year-old man with a diadem, but psychologically, he remained under-developed and immature.

Like many people who feel low self-worth and low self–esteem, Saul was probably unaware of his moment-to-moment emotional shifts. Both conscious and unconscious mental mechanisms are called upon to cope with these deep-seated distressing feelings. In order to ward off these unacceptable feelings, Saul's mind often resorted to unconscious mental mechanisms[4] such as projection (blaming his armies for his fault), denial and rationalization as when he was confronted by Samuel after the battle with the Amalekites. A person with low self-esteem often shows a tendency to rely on others and/or can be easily influenced. Saul was surrounded by people who gave him bad advices. He listened to them and their advices led him to make erroneous judgment. Ironically, a person with low self-esteem often unconsciously seeks out circumstances in the external environment to affirm or justify their feeling of "smallness." Such a person is swift to find faults in others in order to make him feels "bigger." Conversely, when compared to others who actually are bigger in physical stature and who may have more abilities, have greater accomplishments or have more material possessions, the inner voice of such a person may say to himself, "See, I'm really less attractive; I am weak, defective, poor and small." All these feelings arise from having a deep-seated poor image of oneself, the hallmark of a person with low self-esteem and self-worth. The feeling can be devastating to one's ego when one feels publicly humiliated as in the case of Saul when the adorning women compared his achievement with that of David's and he appeared "smaller." (1 Samuel 18:7) He became extremely jealous and furious at David.

To compensate for such feelings of emotional insufficiency, such a person may unconsciously strive to be "number one" at all costs. This type of person comes across as self-centered and self-aggrandized. It is interesting that the scripture described Saul constantly holding a spear on his hand (1 Samuel 18:10; 22:6) as if he needed to show his authority and at the same time, used the weapon to express his aggressive feelings. He devised evil schemes and devoted huge resources to eliminate the one person whom he thought stood in his way to be "number one." Yet, despite one's achievements and successes, this person's gratified feelings may only be transient. Inwardly, an abyss exists that cannot be filled. Furthermore, such a person often lacks insight. Bereft of objective input and the capacity for self-examination, this type may commit serious mistakes as Saul did, with calamitous consequences.

Viewing Saul from this psychological perspective and how he coped with his emotional turmoil, it helps us to gain a fuller picture on how Saul was constantly waging two wars: one without facing his nation and the other within himself. He had his chance to be a great king. But his emotional weakness was an Achilles heel that greatly contributed to his fall from grace. At the end, he lost both battles.

KEY POINTS:

- Saul was the first king of Israel. The establishment of his kingship marked the transition of Israel from a theocratic society to a monarchy.

- Saul's kingship was predicated on observing and keeping the covenantal relationship between Israel and the new king with God.

- Saul was physically impressive. However, psychologically, he seems to have been suffering from low self-esteem.

- Saul had mood disturbances that required music to soothe his feelings.

- Saul's spiritual crises revealed his character flaws and the extent to which he ignored the God's commandments. As a result, the Lord selected another person to succeed him.

- Saul's emotional state spiraled downward from intense jealousy to fear, to paranoia, and finally to homicidal impulses. He committed suicide when he was wounded on the battle field.

- The life of Saul vividly illustrates the inter-play that exists between one's emotional state and one's spirituality.

6. David: Integrity

SIGNIFICANCE:

Maintain integrity. It is the connection to all that is significant in your life.

David

**"Man looks at the outer appearances, but the Lord
looks at the heart."
(1 Samuel 16:7)**

**"I know, my God, that you test the heart and are
pleased with *integrity.*"
(1 Chronicles 29:17)**

Introduction

S amuel was crushed. His chosen man, Saul—young, impressive,
promising, a head taller than any of the Israelis, and whom he
anointed to be the first king of Israel—had disobeyed him and God's
commandments. King Saul did not totally destroy the Amalekites
as Samuel clearly instructed him to do, but spared Agag, their king
and had also spared the best of their animals. Samuel rebuked Saul
by saying, "Because you have rejected the word of the Lord, he
has rejected you as king."(1 Samuel 15:23) Then, Samuel had Agag
brought to him and killed. In one day, Samuel rebuked the king of
Israel and killed the king of the Amalekites. He returned to Ramah
dejected and mourned for Saul a long time as if he had died. Before
his mourning was over, God sent Samuel to Bethlehem to choose
one of Jesse's eight sons to succeed Saul. How would Samuel handle
his assignment this time? Would he make the same mistake again?

As Samuel consecrated Jesse and his sons, he saw Eliab, Jesse's eldest son who impressed Samuel with his appearance and height. But the Lord said to Samuel, "The Lord does not look at the things man looks at. Man looks at the outward appearances, but the Lord looks at the *heart*." (1 Samuel 16:7) The criterion was clear: the Lord wanted someone whose heart would belong to him. Samuel ended up choosing David, Jesse's youngest son, and anointed him the second king of Israel.

David turned out to be a great king. He pacified the surrounding enemies of Israel, expanded the territory, made preparations for the building of the temple of Jerusalem, and chose his son Solomon to succeed him. But David also made grievous mistakes. He committed adultery and murder and tried to cover up his crimes. He abused imperial power. Yet, God still used him in a very important way: Out of his lineage is Christ, the Messiah. What was his *heart* like that made him "the man after God's heart"? What made his life so distinguished? What were the secrets of his success and his redeeming grace?

David

David was "ruddy, with a fine appearance and handsome feature." (1 Samuel 16:12) A shepherd, he had rescued sheep from the jaws of lions and bears. He was articulate and he played the harp well. But most important, "the Lord is with him." (1 Samuel 16:18)

When King Saul was tormented by his mood problems, David was the one brought to Saul's court to play the harp for the king. (1 Samuel 16:14,23; see also Chapter 5) Saul took a liking to him and made him one of his armor-bearers.

Undoubtedly, his early exposure to the political intrigues and infighting that usually came with life in the court gave David invaluable experiences to prepare him to become the future king of Israel. These experiences, plus his fighting abilities, toughened his character and sharpened his survival instincts. Later as king, he demonstrated astute political judgments that saved both his life and his kingdom. His reliance on the Lord was total and he knew how to return to the Lord when he erred. The following selected six episodes of his life reveal his character and spirituality and showed how the "eyes of David's heart" were fixed on the God he loved.

David and Goliath.

David's encounter with Goliath provided the first test of his bravery and prowess in battle. His success made him a hero. It also revealed much of his spirituality. With the armies of the Philistines and Israel facing each other at the Valley of Elah, Goliath, the nine-foot- tall champion from the Philistine camp, challenged the Israelis to select one warrior for man-to-man combat to settle the outcome of the war. For forty mornings and nights, Goliath taunted the Israelites. Finding no one to fight him, the Israelis were dismayed and terrified.

Jesse, David's father, happened to send David to deliver roasted grain and ten loaves of bread to his three older brothers who were with Saul's army and ten cheeses to the commander of their unit. At the front line, David heard Goliath. He asked: "What will be done for the man who kills this Philistine and removes this disgrace from Israel? Who is this uncircumcised Philistine that he should defy the army of the living God?" (1 Samuel 17:26) His conversation with the soldiers was overheard and reported to Saul and Saul sent for him. David convinced Saul to let him fight Goliath.

Skillful and physically strong from years of experience shepherding, David exuded a confidence that stemmed from his strong reliance on the Lord as he faced this nine-foot-tall giant. To David, what was now at stake was more than the might of the Philistine army and the fate of his nation; it dearly mattered to him that the name of the Lord Almighty had been defiled. And in the name of the Lord Almighty, he was going to fight Goliath.

David said to Goliath:

"You come against me with sword and spear and javelin, but I come against you in the name of the Lord Almighty, whom you have defiled. This day, the Lord will hand you over to me...and the whole world will know that there is a God in Israel. All those gathered here will know that it is not by sword or spear that the Lord saves; for the battle is the Lord's, and he will give all of you into our hand." (1 Samuel 17:45-47)

As the combatants moved toward each other, David quickly shot his slingshot at Goliath. The stone hit Goliath in his forehead and most likely sank into his brain. When Goliath fell face down on the ground, he was dead. David ran and stood over him, drew Goliath's sword from the scabbard, and cut off his head. The Philistine army fled and the Israelis routed them that day.

At an early age, David had already held God in total respect. In spite of his skill and bravery, he knew the battle belonged to the Lord. He learned to trust the Lord and rely on the Lord's guidance. His *heart* showed that it belonged to God and the people of Israel. This sentiment would manifest itself repeatedly throughout his life and even during his reign as king. But he was young, and his spirituality had to be tested. His character had to be toughened if he was to rule as king. His relationship with Saul provided the test of his character and spirituality and sharpened his survival instincts.

David and Saul

David's character and spirituality were severely tested by having to face Saul's hostility towards him. How should he respond to a man chosen by God, but who was determined to have him killed?

Saul had initially taken a liking to David, made him his harpist and one of his armor-bearers. Saul had witnessed his bravery and prowess against Goliath and realized the triumph and glory that David had brought him that day. But Saul's perception of David changed immediately after he heard the refrain of the women's chorus: "Saul has slain his thousands and David his tens of thousands." (see Chapter 5). This refrain bothered Saul and he became very angry with David. And from that day on, Saul's sentiment turned against David and he "kept a jealous eye on David." (1 Samuel 18:9) Saul's rapid change of mood and perception of David revealed how insecure he was. Unknowingly, David had been drawn into a conflict with Saul where he must decide what to do with God's chosen king who was determined to have him killed.

Feeling insecure, Saul ordered David killed. He initially plotted to have David killed at the hands of the Philistines, asking for the foreskins of a hundred Philistines in exchange for the marriage to his daughter Michal. David came back with two hundred. When the plot failed and Saul realized that the Lord was with David, and that Michal loved David, as did all Israel, he became even more fearful of David. Twice he erupted with anger and tried to pin David against the wall with his spear. David escaped unharmed and fled. Initially, David was baffled by Saul's murderous intent as he had done nothing to provoke the king's anger. After realizing Saul was intent on having him killed, David escaped for good. He found various hiding places in the Judean desert and the surrounding areas. But Saul hunted him like "a partridge in the mountain" and a "flea."

Twice, David had the opportunity to kill Saul. The first opportunity came at a cave along the way to the Crags of the Wild Goats in the Desert of En Gedi. Saul went into a cave to relieve himself, not realizing that David and his men were hiding at the back of the cave. David crept up unnoticed and cut off a corner of Saul's robe. For this, David was "conscience-stricken." He said to his men, "The Lord forbid that I should do such a thing to my master, *the Lord's anointed*, or lift up my hand against him; for he is *the anointed of the Lord*." (1 Samuel 24:6)

The second opportunity was in the Desert of Ziph, where David and his men were staying. Saul had led three thousand men in pursuit of David. Saul's army encamped beside the road on the hill of Hakilah facing Jeshimon. While Saul was sleeping inside the camp with his spear stuck in the ground near his head and with Abner, his commander and his soldiers lying asleep around him, David and Abishai, his warrior, sneaked up on him at night. Finding Saul, Abishai wanted to kill him. But David said to him: "Don't destroy him! Who can lay a hand on *the Lord's anointed* and be guiltless? As surely as the Lord lives, the Lord himself will strike him; either his time will come and he will die, or he will go into battle and perish. But the Lord forbids that I should lay a hand on *the Lord's anointed*..." (1 Samuel 26:9-11)

Regardless of how evil Saul's intentions were toward him, and how vengeful Saul's murderous intent might have made David feel, David repeatedly forbade the killing of Saul, *the Lord's anointed*. Although he could not understand the reasons behind Saul's motive to kill him and had all the right reasons for revenge, David's spiritual eyes made him override his vengeful feelings toward Saul. He respected the Lord's decision and design in choosing Saul as the first king of Israel. He wasn't going to allow himself or any person to raise his hand to dishonor God by killing his *anointed*. His feeling toward Saul was not going to be "an eye for an eye." David did not seek personal revenge. He trusted God to deal with his chosen person in his own way and time. God's will and not his personal feelings were to guide his actions in dealing with the Lord's chosen even though Saul had misunderstood him and wanted him killed.

David and Mephibosheth

How David treated Jonathan's surviving son revealed his magnanimity and his integrity. David and Jonathan, Saul's son, formed an abiding friendship and love. When David was fleeing from Saul, Jonathan asked David to take an oath to show kindness to his family. (1 Samuel 20:14-15) With his ascension to kingship, David asked, "Is there anyone still left of the house of Saul to whom I can show kindness for Jonathan's sake?" (2 Samuel 9:1) Mephibosheth, Jonathan's crippled son, was reported to be the only survivor. David sent for him and restored to him all the land that belonged to King Saul. He invited Mephibosheth to eat at his table. (2 Samuel 9:7) David also ordered Ziba, Saul's servant, and Ziba's household and servants to provide for Mephibosheth.

In his treatment of Mephibosheth, David showed that he was a man of his word. He kept his vow with Jonathan. His character exuded mercy. His dealing with Saul's grandson is reminiscent of how God showed mercy toward his chosen people. Despite the fact that God's chosen people had rebelled against him and had broken his covenant, God kept his promise. Just as David showed mercy to the crippled Mephibosheth, God elevated the poor and the lowly. Though undeserving, Mephiboseth was treated as a member of David's family, a beautiful illustration of God's love. David's love for Jonathan, his integrity, and his spirituality in his dealing with Mephibosheth epitomized God's heart in dealing with his people.

David and Bathsheba

David's spirituality faced a severe crisis at the height of his success. Sex, murder, the attempt to cover-up his sin and his abuse of imperial power almost brought him down. His spirituality was the one redeeming factor. Although the immediate consequence of his adulterous relation with Bathsheba caused the death of their first son, their second son, Solomon became the builder of the temple of God. What is the spiritual message behind the story between David and Bathsheba? And how did this reflect David's spirituality?

When Joab and the entire Israeli army were fighting the Ammonites and besieging Rabbah, David remained in Jerusalem. While walking around the roof of his palace one evening, David saw the beautiful Bathsheba bathing. He was enticed and then sent for her. In a lapse of judgment, David went to bed with Bathsheba and she became pregnant. (2 Samuel 11:2-5)

To cover up his sin, David sent for Uriah, Bathsheba's husband, who was with Joab's army fighting the Ammonites. David schemed to have Uriah brought back from the frontline to sleep with his wife to cover up his sin. But the plot failed. When he returned, out of a sense of patriotism and loyalty to his commander Joab and his fellow soldiers, Uriah refused to go home and sleep with his wife. Then David schemed to have him killed at the frontline of battle. After Uriah's death, David brought Bathsheba to be his wife.

His adultery and murderous act greatly displeased the Lord. The Lord sent the prophet Nathan to confront David about his sinful act: he had despised the word of the Lord by doing what is evil in the Lord's eyes. As a consequence, Nathan pronounced that the sword will never depart from David's house. (2 Samuel 12: 9-10) What he had done in secret will be reciprocated by someone close to him who will shame him by taking his wives and lie with them in broad daylight. (2 Samuel 12:11-12)

David realized that he had committed grievous sins. His admittance of his sins against the Lord was swift and sincere. He was truly remorseful. Unlike Saul's equivocated response to Samuel when he sinned, David's utterance of "I have sinned" was sincere and contrite. He assumed total responsibility for his error and his lapse of judgment.

Although the Lord spared his life and did not strip David of his kingship as he did with Saul, David was to suffer greatly for his offenses. The immediate result was the death of the child born to him. Calamity ruled in David's household and there was no peace.

The unfolding of God's punishment and divine justice revealed that subsequently, Amnon, David's son, fell in love with Tamar, the beautiful sister of Absalom. He lured her to his room, raped and disgraced her. Enraged, two years later, Absalom plotted and had Amnon killed and then fled to Geshur. David was devastated. He mourned Amnon and his heart longed for Absalom. Realizing how much David's heart was with Absalom, Joab planned to have Absalom brought back to Jerusalem. But Absalom had changed. Upon his return to Jerusalem, Absalom started to conspire against his father. After four years, when he had marshaled enough forces, Absalom marched to overtake Jerusalem. David quickly fled with his officers, family and men. Upon entering Jerusalem, Absalom openly laid with David's concubines on the roof of the palace "in the sight of all Israel" thus fulfilling Nathan's prophesies. (2 Samuel 16:22) David's escape from Jerusalem was a dark moment in his luminous career as king.

The story of David and Bathsheba showed that even a person as strong and faithful to God as David could err. His action brought calamities to his family, shame to his kingdom and his Lord. He almost lost his kingship. But there is a redeeming quality in David's character. When he made a mistake, he was contrite and he assumed total responsibility. He was able to look straight at his sinful acts, confess them and fervently pray for forgiveness and renewal of his spirit. In Psalms 51 which David composed after the prophet Nathan had confronted him, he revealed his deep pain and agony:

> Have mercy on me, O God,
> according to your unfailing love;
> according to your great compassion
> blot out my transgressions.
> Wash away all my iniquity
> And cleanse me from my sin. (Psalms 51:1-2)

But David's spiritual eyes saw another aspect of God in his prayer:

The sacrifices of God are a broken spirit;
a broken and contrite heart,
O God, you will not despise. (Psalms 51:17)

Psalm 51 revealed David's insight and understanding of God's heart. Unlike Saul's equivocating manner of confession, David was truly remorseful. He took the necessary steps to be restored and be renewed after he stumbled. Crushed by the guilt of his sins, he knew that if he repented, God would show mercy. David kept faith in God.

But that did not relieve him of the need to manage the immediate crisis facing his nation and his kingship. Although he was resigned to receive whatever God wanted to do with him even if it meant death for him and his family, he still had to exercise judgment and take actions to save his kingdom. In the darkest moments of his kingship, he still trusted God. He was never just a passive follower of God's will. He actively prayed for the Lord's guidance and wisdom. He asked God to frustrate the advice of his traitor/adviser, Ahithophel to Absalom. He actively worked to restore his relation with God. Then, he took actions to overcome the scheme of his enemies. In whatever he did, God was preeminent in his mind and heart.

The spiritual message is clear: repent and God will forgive. The way David took action provided a contrast to the way the Israelites responded to God's plea generations later: "Come, let us reason together, though your sins are like scarlet, they shall be as white as snow. Though they red as crimson, they shall be like wool." (Isaiah 1:18) The Israelites refused to repent and their recalcitrant hearts led to the demise of their kingdom. David responded positively and he was restored. The all merciful God realized the frailty of man's spirituality and human nature. It is only when our faith is anchored in God that it can serve as a bulwark against sinfulness and a source of redemption when we sin. When we stumble and fall, God will extend his hands and lift us up if we are willing to reach out to him.

David and Shimei

How should we treat our enemies and those who cause us trouble when we're down? What did David's spiritual eyes see in his interaction with Shimei?

One of the saddest and most humiliating moments in King David's reign was the insult he received from Shimei as he was fleeing from his son Absalom. Shimei was the son of Gera who came from the tribe of Benjamin, the same clan as Saul's family. As David and all his troops and special guard were approaching Bahurim, Shimei came out, started to curse and insult David and pelted David and all the king's officials with stone. (2 Samuel 16:6) Shimei said, "Get out, get out, you man of blood, you scoundrel! The Lord has repaid you for all the blood you shed in the household of Saul, in whose place you have reigned. The Lord has handed the kingdom over to your son Absalom. You have come to ruin because you are a man of blood!" (2 Samuel 16:7-8) Shimei was rubbing salt into David's emotional wounds. Enraged, Abishai, David's warrior, wanted to kill Shimei. But David said, "If he is cursing because the Lord said to him, 'Curse David,' who can ask, 'Why do you do this?'" He added, "Leave him alone; let him curse, for the Lord has told him to. It may be that the Lord will see in my distress and repay me with good for the cursing I am receiving today." (2 Samuel 16:11-12)

David knew that God was speaking to him through Shimei, to teach him a lesson. In every circumstance David was in, even in extreme situations, David was tuned into God's voice. David could easily have succumbed to his anger and had the head of Shimei cut off as requested by Abishai. But he restrained himself. Instead, he tried to listen to God's "gentle whisper" while in the midst of fire. To David, Shimei's curse was a gentle reminder of God's message for him: keep calm; be patient; and that it was senseless to shed the blood of a defenseless man. He had to keep his equanimity at a critical moment facing his kingship and life. The big picture was unfolding in Jerusalem. At that moment, David was wondering whether his friend Hushai whom he had sent back to Jerusalem, would be able to frustrate the advice of Ahithophel, his adviser who had turned against him and sided with Absalom.

Ahithophel had advised Absalom to attack David that night while he was "weary and weak." But Hushai urged Absalom to wait and gather more troops to fight David. Absalom and his men sided with Hushai. This gave Hushai time to inform David to quickly lead his men across over the Jordan River and regroup. Then David mustered his men at Mehanaim to face Absalom and his troops. At the battle in the forest of Ephraim, David's troops killed twenty thousand of Absalom's men. Absalom, while riding his mule, had his head caught in the thick branches of a large oak. Joab, defying the king's order not to harm Absalom, had him killed. David's kingship was saved.

When David was being welcome back to Jerusalem by the men of Judah, Shimei was among the first of the house of Joseph to cross over the Jordan to greet David. He pleaded with David to forgive him. Again, Abishai asked to kill Shimei for his cursing the "Lord's anointed." David refused. On the day he restored his kingship, he wasn't going to allow any more people to be killed in Israel.

David knew that Shimei couldn't be trusted and could cause future trouble for Solomon. Years later, when Solomon was king and David was old, he warned Solomon about Shimei and mentioned what Shimei had done to him. (1 Kings 2:8-9) He trusted Solomon to deal wisely with Shimei. (Solomon confined Shimei to Jerusalem and warned him that he would die if he left the city and crossed the Kidron Valley. Shimei agreed. Three years later, when Shimei violated the king's order and went to Gath to seek his runaway slaves and bring them back to Jerusalem, Solomon had him killed.)

David spared Shimei's life, twice, just as he had twice spared King Saul's life. He knew how to restrain his anger. It was not just a matter of exacting vengeance. The bigger picture was the Lord's message and will. David could discern spiritual messages in the midst of danger and in the heat of passion. He knew that "vengeance belonged to the Lord" and he left it to the Lord to exact vengeance. He accepted reality. He was politically astute and correctly assessed each situation he faced against his enemies. In the midst of adversarial situations, David sought to discern God's will. Where adversity may cause others to falter, panic, fail, or become vengeful, it only strengthened David emotionally and spiritually. He emerged a stronger person because the eyes of his heart clearly saw the heart of God and he resonated with it.

David made preparations to build the Temple of Jerusalem

David's decision in choosing the site of the Lord's temple revealed the depth and insight of his spirituality. The symbolism attached to the events that prompted David to choose the "Araunah's threshing floor" to be the site for God's temple reflected his keen spiritual eyes. Near the conclusion of his life, how did he manage his ambitions when these clashed with God's will?

David yearned to have the ark of God brought to Jerusalem. He had conferred with each of his officers and commanders and the whole assembly of Israel and they all agreed with his wish to bring the ark of God to Jerusalem. (1 Chronicles 13:4) But the process leading to the decision to determine the site to build the temple of God turned out to be a severe test of David's spirituality. The path was filled with spiritual obstacles. Initially, the ark was moved from the house of Abinadab in Kiriath Jearim. Because the movers did not follow God's prescribed way to move the ark by Levites who had consecrated themselves in order to carry the ark of God with poles on their shoulders, as Moses had commanded them, the Lord "broke out in anger" against them. (1 Chronicles 15:13) The oxen carrying the ark stumbled. Uzzah reached out his hand to steady the ark and for touching the ark, he was struck down by God. David became afraid and wondered whether he ever could bring the ark of God to Jerusalem. Instead of bringing it to Jerusalem as originally intended, David had the ark taken to the house of Obed-Edom and it remained there for three months.

Then David prepared a place for the ark of God and pitched a tent for it after he had constructed buildings for himself in the city of David. The second time around, the arrangement for carrying the ark was done in the proper, prescribed way and carried by conse-crated Levites. The ark was brought into the city of David amidst much fanfare and celebration and was placed in the tent David had pitched for it.

But David's heart still yearned to have a permanent temple build for the ark. And the site for the ark had yet to be determined.

Meanwhile, David had ordered the taking of a census of the fighting men of Israel and Judah. To the modern reader, the taking of a national census as a function of government may seem innocuous. But the event precipitated a momentous and costly crisis for David and the nation of Israel. After David had received the census, he was conscience-stricken. What appeared to be a routine governmental function in census taking turned out to be a grievous sin in God's eyes. David quickly realized it: "I have sinned greatly in what I have done." (2 Samuel 24:10) David realized that he had done a very foolish thing in the sight of God and in Israel and he knew he was guilty. His action greatly displeased God. It was an act so grievous that God sent the Prophet Gad to give the king three options to choose from as his punishment:

1. Three years of famine
2. Three days of pestilence
3. Three months during which David would flee before enemies and be overtaken by the sword (2 Samuel 24:13; 1 Chronicles 21:12)

It was a choice that tormented David. David chose not to fall into the hands of men. (2 Samuel 24:14) So God sent a plague over Israel that killed seventy thousand people.

What could have possibly gone wrong?

We are left with no clear explanation as to why the taking of the census was anathema to God. Clearly, there were layers of deeper spiritual meanings attending such an act that provoked such a divine anger and that plunged David's spirituality and the kingdom of Israel into this crisis. For David, his spirituality was being tested again just as it was tested when he went to bed with Bathsheba. He uttered the same confession, "I have sinned." Beyond the conjecture that the census may have provided the King the means of "imposing the hated burden of conscription and taxation on the populace," [1] I am inclined to surmise that David had again abused his imperial authority by flaunting his "ego" and power as other earthly kings had done. From a deeper spiritual perspective, David had deviated from the covenantal relationship with God that he had painstakingly kept to sustain his kingship.

The census was conducted for the first time after David had consolidated his imperial power. Most of his traitors, including Sheba had either been neutralized or eliminated. He had made peace with the Gibeonites. David's armies had pacified the Philistines. "The Lord delivered him from all his enemies and from the hand of Saul." (2 Samuel 22:1) He had at his command mighty men and commanders that could easily be the envy of any nation. He knew God was on his side. He was confident that God was his rock, his fortress and his deliverer. (2 Samuel 22:2) He had scrupulously consulted God before he had embarked on his previous battles, and he knew that the outcome of the battle belonged to the Lord.

There was really no need for him to know the number of his fighting men by taking a census. Even Joab, the commander-in-chief of his army questioned the wisdom of such a decision: "May the Lord your God multiply the troops a hundred times over, and may the *eyes* of my lord the king *see* it. But why does my lord the king want to do such a thing?" (2 Samuel 24:3)

I believe that the *eyes of the heart* of David which had heretofore exclusively focused on God in times of battle now had shifted the focus to himself in times of peace. For the first time, he wanted to "see" and to "know" the extent of his army, the extent of his imperial power. His spiritual eyes temporarily turned from a reliance on the Almighty God to a reliance on his earthly power. Joab knew better and told him that God could have multiplied his troops a hundred times over, and that his *eyes* could *see* it. But David wouldn't listen. His spiritual eyes were temporarily blinded. In an episode that is reminiscence of his wandering *eyes* when he saw the naked and beautiful Bathsheba, David's eyes now focused on himself, his ego. He behaved like other earthly kings who had assumed absolute power. In this instance, he again abused his power and caused hardship on his armies and on the people of Israel. His spirituality had deviated from God and moved closer to the kind of arrogance that had caused the downfall of King Saul. He was violating the very covenant that God had established with the kingship over Israel. That was unacceptable to God. And so God had to teach him a grave lesson. His people suffered tremendously for his mistake; God sent the plague that killed seventy thousand of David's people. And the sword of the angel of the Lord was ready to strike Jerusalem.

As the sword of the angel of the Lord was at the threshing floor of Araunah the Jebusite, and his hand had stretched out and ready to destroy Jerusalem, God grieved over the calamity that had befallen his people. He ordered the angel to withdraw his hand. The temporary respite gave David a chance to seek atonement. When David saw the angel striking down the people, his heart as the great shepherd and king was moved. He said to the Lord, "I am the one who has sinned and done wrong. These are but sheep. What have they done? Let your hand fall upon me and my family." (2 Samuel 24:17) Here, the shepherd of his flock pleaded to save his sheep at the site of the threshing floor and he was ready to sacrifice his life and his family for it. David had returned to his true self as the shepherd of his flock.

God gave David a second chance and sent Gad to reveal to him the path to atonement—to build an altar to the Lord on the threshing floor of Araunah the Jebusite. (2 Samuel 24:18) Because David's heart had wandered away from the covenant of God, he must return to the ritual of the covenant to restore his relation with God and with his people. God again demanded the exclusive devotion of his subject and his people. The eyes of the king's heart must fixate on God again. But the threshing floor where sacrifices were offered still belonged to Araunah.

As king, he could have easily take the threshing floor, but David had learned his lesson. He offered to pay the full price for the purchase of the site. He was not going to offer burnt offerings to God that cost him nothing. (2 Samuel 24:24) This time around, he did not abuse his power.

So, David bought the threshing floor, built an altar there and sacrificed burnt offering and fellowship offerings. "Then the Lord answered the prayers and the plague on Israel was stopped." (2 Samuel 24:25) The covenantal relationship was restored.

When David saw the Lord had answered his call, he determined that the site of the temple would be *at* the threshing floor of Araunah the Jebusite.

Thus, the site for the ark of the covenant of God was chosen and bought at a high price, both in financial and human terms. This rite is filled with deep spiritual meanings. On the threshing floor, the drama between David, the Israelites, the angel and God played out. There, the sword of the angel, ready to destroy Jerusalem because of David's sin was halted. God grieved over the calamity brought on his people. David pleaded; God responded. An altar was built and on it, David offered sacrifices and God responded approvingly. God answered David's call. The plague ended. Both David's relationship with God and that of his people's relationship with God were restored. With the site for the temple of God chosen, a dangerous saga ended that could have seriously tainted David's career. All signs pointed to the threshing floor as the spot where the relationship between God and man was reconciled; where the heart of man and God were to touch each other; and where love was to triumph over justice. Man had repented his sins and God had relented on his anger. Man became obedient and God showed mercy. Man offered sacrifices and God gladly accepted them. God had ensured that the site for his temple was to be cleansed of all uncleanness in order to reflect his mercy, to be a place of peace and rest and for the offering of supreme sacrifices. David understood all of this when he decided on the site—"The house of the Lord *is* to be here, and also the altar of burnt offering for Israel." (1 Chronicles 22:1)

Still, the ark was under a tent. He had a consuming desire to build a house for the ark of the covenant of the Lord. He said to the prophet Nathan, "Here I am, living in a palace of cedar, while the ark of the covenant of Lord is under a tent." That night God revealed his words in a dream to the prophet Nathan: David was *not* to be the person to build the temple. God was going to raise up one of his sons to build it. (1 Chronicles 17:11-12)

Nathan reported his dream to David. David's response to the Lord showed no hint of disappointment despite his consuming desire to build the temple for the Lord. All of his adult life, he would have loved to cap his career with the crowning achievement as the builder of the dwelling for God. After all, he had interacted with God in the most intimate and personal way, through thick and thin during his entire career. Nathan's report of his dream to David tested again David's spirituality. Was he willing to relinquish his personal ambition, his narcissism, to be remembered as the person who built the Temple of God when the opportunity was so close? David humbled himself and responded by completely accepting the Lord's revelation and instructions. In his prayer, he said:

Who am I, O Lord, and what is my family, that you have brought me this far? And as if this were not enough in your sight, O God, you have spoken about the future of the house of your servant....You, my God, have revealed to your servant that you will build a house for him. So your servant has found courage to pray to you. O Lord, you are God! You have promised these good things to your servant. Now you have been pleased to bless the house of your servant, that it may continue forever in your sight; for you, O Lord, have blessed it, and it will be blessed forever. (1 Chronicles 17:16-17, 25-27)

By totally submitting to God's will, the man whose heart belonged to God, in turn, was told by God that God would build a house for him and that it will live forever.[2] What a privilege and an honor! But in his old age, he had to give up his ego. The name of his son, not his name, would be associated with the building of the Temple forever.

So David made extensive preparations for the temple before his death. He charged his son, Solomon to build it. David assembled all the officers, commanders, and soldiers in the sight of all Israel and of the Assembly of God and charged them to carefully follow all the commands of the Lord so that they may possess their land and pass it on as an inheritance to their descendants forever. (1 Chronicles 28:8)

To Solomon, his son, he urged him to acknowledge God and serve him with wholehearted devotion and with a willing mind. (1 Chronicles 28:9).

Above and beyond everything that David already had materially prepared for the building of the temple, David willingly gave his personal treasures of gold and silver. The people responded in kind, and collectively gave even more. (1 Chronicles 29:9)

David's parting prayer was:

> ...I know my God that you test the heart and are pleased with *integrity*. All these things have I given willingly and with honest intent. And now I have *seen* with joy how willingly your people who are here have given to you. O Lord, God of our fathers Abraham, Isaac and Israel, keep this *desire in the hearts* of your people forever, and keep their *hearts* loyal to you. (1 Chronicles 29:17-18)

Conclusion

What was David's heart like in his relationship to God and his people? In battles, he was brave. He relied on God and wasn't going to allow God's name to be defiled. In dealing with others, even with his enemies, he was forgiving and fair. To his friends, he kept his promises and was a man of his word. He had integrity. He showed kindness to the downtrodden. In administration, he was wise. Politically, he was astute and knew how to surround himself with the best, the most loyal, and the wisest.

His heart was always tuned into God's will and it belonged to his people. His intimate understanding of the heart of God was most impressive and was akin to that of his relationship to Jonathan. He fully trusted the Lord — in battle and during the depth of his suffering, misery and sorrow. In the midst of crises and adversities, he kept his spiritual ear opened to and the eyes of his heart focused on the messages from God. Where others may have faltered and retreated, his faith in God grew stronger and his spirituality soared to new heights. In repentance, in love, in kindness, in worship and sacrifices, and in giving, he set the standard of integrity and an example for all Israeli to follow. God was pre-eminent in his heart. At his best, David was the ideal king. Truly, David was a man after God's heart.

KEY POINTS:

- David was chosen to succeed Saul as "a man after the heart of God."

- David's spiritual eyes were keenly focused on God. When he made mistakes, he was contrite. His repentance was swift and thorough. He returned to God immediately.

- David knew that the Lord wanted to test his heart and check his integrity.

- The story of David is one of repentance and forgiveness; of human transgressions and divine grace; of God's redemption and love.

- Man looks at the outer appearances but God looks at the heart.

- God desires offerings given out of a willing heart.

- God insists that the temple wherein he dwells must be absolutely holy.

- David's heart was constantly attuned to God.

- As a true test of his spirituality, David is willing to sacrifice himself and his family to atone for his sins and spare his people of the sufferings he had caused.

- David is human. What makes him exceptional was his insight into God, his respect for God, his integrity, his willingness to genuinely repent and to accept God's will over his life.

7. Jonah: Character Flaws

SIGNIFICANCE:

Correct your character flaws. It will enhance your effectiveness as a person and increase your job satisfaction.

Jonah

**"Those who cling to worthless idols forfeit the grace
that could be theirs."
(Jonah 2:8)**

Introduction

Jonah sat silently in a hurriedly patched-up hut he built for himself, to shield himself from the merciless, sweltering sun. His eyes burned at Nineveh, that imposing and teeming city he would rather forget. For three days he had walked in it and monotonously warned the inhabitants of its destruction. It didn't matter that the king, who, upon hearing Jonah's proclamation, "rose from his throne, took off his royal robes, covered himself with sackcloth, sat down in the dust" (Jonah 3:6) and ordered a proclamation to his subjects to follow his example of sincere repentance. Jonah would rather have seen the Ninevites go along in their previous way. That would fit perfectly with the fate he thought they justly deserved—to die. This mission he truly loathed. It was against his grain, his logic, his values and his beliefs for him, a Jew, to preach to the gentiles, his nation's enemy. Worse, he felt betrayed by God. For trying what he thought was a justified escapade, he had gone through three days and three nights of pure hell—bouncing in the belly of a big fish, struggling to keep his head above the engulfing waters, gasping for breath, and frantically trying to tear off the seaweed that had wrapped around his head like a tightening noose. And, God did that for what purpose? To fulfill a mission that Jonah predicted that God, Himself, would relent on, that God would stop threatening the city and spare the city from destruction? It made no sense to him. Jonah thought he knew better than God. He burned with anger at God. It didn't matter to him that he was arguing with his Creator. He wasn't about to respond to the gentle voice of God about his *right* to be angry. Of course, he thought he had the *rights* to be angry! He had had it. "Destroy Nineveh or let me die." Jonah fumed as he sat on the sand. He kept his eyes squarely on Nineveh and wanted to see if the Lord would rain down burning sulfur as he had done to Sodom and Gomorrah.

What kind of a prophet was Jonah that he was so angry at God for sparing the city God threatened to destroy? What accounted for this mood and his actions? Why did he plead for his own death at the height of his success in his life? What does this say about his spirituality?

Background

Little is known about the prophet Jonah, 800-750 BC. He was the son of Amittai, the prophet from Gath Hepher. Jonah ministered during the reign of Jeroboam II, 793-753 BC, of the Northern Kingdom of Israel. His contemporary was the Prophet Amos, 760-750 BC. The prophet Elisha, 847-797, BC lived before him. He lived at a time which saw the emergence of Assyria as an aggressive world power. Damascus, her northern neighbor, had continued its border dispute with Israel. Jonah had predicted the restoration of Israel's northern boundary to King Jeroboam II (2 Kings 14:25) and the king's military successes included the recovery for Israel of both Damascus and Hamath. (2 Kings 14:28) But the restoration of the political boundary of Israel and the resurgence of her prosperity were short-lived. In 722 BC, three decades after Jonah's death, Assyria (900-605 BC) would conquer and absorb the Northern Kingdom of Israel. It was within this historical context that God sent Jonah to call the people of Nineveh, the capital of Assyria, located along the bank of the Tigris River, to repentance.

Jonah

God said to His prophet Jonah, "Go to the great city of Nineveh and preach against it, because its wickedness has come up before me." (Jonah 1:2) This assignment was unacceptable to Jonah. Instead of going east to Nineveh, he boarded a ship sailing west toward Tarshish, in the direction of Spain. As a result of his rebellion, the ship encountered a ferocious storm that threatened to break it up. While all the sailors frantically threw the cargo overboard to lighten the ship, Jonah slept soundly on the lower deck. The pounding of the wind and the sea was unrelenting. The sailors cried out to their gods, but received no answer. In desperation, the captain awoke Jonah and said, "How can you sleep? Get up and call on your god! Maybe he will take notice of us, and we will not perish." Then the sailors cast lots to find out who was responsible for bringing this calamity. When the lot fell on Jonah, they wanted to know his identity and who this man was who had caused all this trouble. They already knew that Jonah was running away from the Lord because he had told them that much when he boarded the ship. But they did not realize the enormity and significance of Jonah's disobedience. When Jonah told them that he was a Hebrew who worships "the Lord, God of heaven, who made the sea and the land" this only terrified them. This God who controlled the sea and the land was showing his fury and they were stuck with Jonah, the man who claimed to have a special relationship with this living God and possibly held the key to their deliverance. And yet, they had found him sound asleep while the storm raged!

> "What should we do to you to make the sea calm down for us?" they asked.
> "Pick me up and throw me into the sea and it will become calm," Jonah replied. "I know that it is my fault that this great storm has come upon you." (Jonah 1:12)

Jonah's nonchalant, straight-forward response must have puzzled the sailors. He seemed resigned to his fate. But the sailors could not bring themselves to throw an innocent person into the sea. They tried hard to row back to land. But when "the sea grew even wilder than before," they had no choice but to throw Jonah overboard. Grief-stricken, they all cried out to their newly-found God and pleaded with him not to be held accountable for killing Jonah. They acknowledged, "For you O Lord, have done as you pleased." Then they reluctantly threw Jonah overboard and the "raging sea grew calm." "At this the men greatly feared the Lord, and they offered a sacrifice to the Lord and made vows to him." (Jonah 1:16)

Like a prelude to an orchestral theme, the episode at sea unfurled the central motifs in the book of Jonah: God's sovereignty, justice and compassion; his desire for the people of the world to repent, and for his servants to change and be transformed into more effective instruments. On God's scale of values, mercy triumphs over justice. The stormy crisis at sea is only a preliminary test of Jonah's spirituality. But the contrast between Jonah's behavior, a prophet of God, and that of the gentile sailors is stark and telling:

1. God revealed his fury through the storm. In the midst of the calamity, Jonah was asleep while the sailors worked furiously to save the ship.
2. Jonah, who professed to know the living God that ruled the sea, did not pray to calm the sea. Rather, it was the gentile sailors, who found the living God through the confession of Jonah, who prayed to the living Lord for forgiveness.
3. Jonah did not seem to care about the fate of the ship, the sailors or himself. The sailors, in turn, tried everything to save Jonah and the ship. The converted gentiles showed more mercy and compassion than the man of God!
4. Jonah rebelled against God's command. The converted sailors acknowledged that the Lord absolutely had the right to do as he pleased.

The Prelude

When Jonah was determined to run away from his calling, the Lord wanted Jonah to stop, listen, and discern what his messages were for him. God's messages were conveyed in the fury of the wind and sea and in the behavior of the sailors. But the "eyes of the heart" of Jonah were too "blind" to see. He was too consumed by his own assumptions about what God should do. Jonah knew that he was the cause of the calamity that befell the ship and he did nothing to save it. Paradoxically, through Jonah's confession, redemption had come to the sailors as they turned from their gods to the living God. Very early, God was telling Jonah to change his ways, to repent, to change his course of action and to obey his commands. God wanted Jonah to see that God was merciful, in addition to being just. He was waiting for Jonah to open the eyes of his heart. It was as if God was telling Jonah: "Look at the sailors. Though they had every right to throw you overboard, they tried to save you and had pleaded for mercy on your behalf. If you had repented as they did, I could have spared you all these troubles. For I, the Lord, will show mercy." Through the compassion of the sailors, God was revealing an aspect of himself that Jonah had much difficulty grasping. Jonah didn't realize that God not only cared about the people of Nineveh, God also was vitally interested in the sailors and in him—to transform him into a better instrument. But Jonah was too wrapped up with his own ego.

So God prepared a big fish that swallowed Jonah, and Jonah spent three days and three nights in the fish's belly fighting for his life. He had to be brought to a near-death experience to confront his character flaws. His stubbornness, callous heart, self-centeredness and lack of insight into God had to change if he was to become an effective instrument of God. In the depth of his misery, he finally called upon the Lord:

> "You hurled me into the deep, into the very heart of the seas." (Jonah 2:3)
> "I have been banished from your sight; yet I will look again toward your holy temple." (Jonah 2:4)
> "But you brought my life up from the pit, O Lord my God." (Jonah 2:6)
> "But I, with a song of thanksgiving, will sacrifice to you. What I have vowed I will make good. Salvation comes from the Lord." (Jonah 2:9)

And in a statement that almost appeared out of context, Jonah said, "Those who cling to worthless idols forfeit the grace that could be theirs." (Jonah 2:8) What were Jonah's idols? Did he suddenly gain insight and realize that the path to God's grace meant that he had to lay down his idols? Did his subconscious catch a glimpse of his stubbornness, rebelliousness, and narcissism[1] that almost caused his death? Did the experience at the sea teach him a lesson of the heart? Did he come to realize that God is compassionate as well as just? Did he fully understand and accept that "salvation comes from the Lord?" Above all, through all the turbulence that swelled around him, did he realize that God still cared very much about him and that he wanted Jonah to change just as he wanted Nineveh to repent?

The test

The Lord answered Jonah's prayer by commanding the fish to vomit him onto dry land. God gave him a second chance. And this time, Jonah's preaching led to the repentance of the entire city of Nineveh. They all believed in the living God. Ninevites's sincerity and acts of repentance moved God's heart:

> "When the Lord saw what they did and how they turned from their evil ways, he had compassion and did not bring upon them the destruction he had threatened." (Jonah 3:10)

This would have been the perfect place to conclude Jonah's life mission. The scene of a repentant prophet leading a whole population of gentiles to salvation couldn't have been more picture-perfect. Yet, the book of Jonah didn't end there. The man who acknowledged that "salvation belongs to the Lord," still had unresolved psychological and spiritual issues to reckon with. Ironically, Jonah's successful mission only revealed his true self and his character flaw. His simmering anger erupted into a full, open, frontal confrontation with God.

God's reversal of his decision to destroy the city of Nineveh greatly displeased Jonah. He was furious. He argued with God and demanded to know God's motives. If God had already known the outcome of Nineveh's action, just as Jonah had anticipated before he had run away, why did God put him through all these troubles? Jonah would have stomped on the floor of heaven to make his point: "Now, O Lord, take away my life, for it is better for me to die than to live." He left God with two alternatives—his death or the destruction of Nineveh. Jonah left the city, and sat in the burning desert sand to see what God would do.

Jonah had to be brought to his senses. The near-death experiences in the belly of the fish had not pierced through the thick armor of his character shield and self-centeredness. It's either his way or death. Since he forced his hand on God by issuing an ultimatum to God, the issue now is no longer with Nineveh, but now centers on Jonah's attitude, his assumptions about God, and his own character traits. All through his crises, Jonah still hadn't realized, as the sailors did, that God is both compassionate and righteous and that he has the absolute *right* to do what he pleases. God's wonderful design was beyond what Jonah's intelligence could fathom. Wasn't it God's providence that through Jonah's rebellion, the sailors had come to believe in the living God? Didn't God show him, through the actions of the sailors, a foretaste of what His compassion was? And could he be able to realize the divine's foretelling that his three days and three nights in the belly of the fish were a foreshadowing of Christ's death and burial for three days before the resurrection? (Matthew 12:40) Doesn't salvation belong to God and doesn't *he* actualize it to change the attitudes and hearts of men, just as he did with the Ninevites? When would Jonah be able to connect his heart to his intellect?

The final confrontation

Jonah's behavior called into question what he professed to believe. If Jonah had truly believed that "salvation comes from the Lord" as he had articulated in the belly of the fish, why was he still so angry? Jonah was grateful that God spared his life. He had tasted the mercy of God. He was empowered again to preach the word of God. But why couldn't he fathom the depth of God's compassion and why did he keep insisting that God should destroy Nineveh? Why did Jonah, who knew and experienced first-hand the power of the Lord ruler of the sea and land, challenge the ultimate authority and motives of God? The issue with Jonah lay deep within his psyche—his self-centeredness and his narcissism.

To confront Jonah's narcissism, God provided him with a vine that shaded his head from the burning sun. Jonah loved it. For the first time, he was happy. In the midst of his misery, he experienced God's comfort in a loving, intimate, and physical way. The next day, God introduced a worm to chew down the vine and Jonah lost the only personal comfort left in his life and that made him furious. Then God sent a scorching east wind and a blazing sun that beat down on Jonah's head. He became delirious. And in this totally miserable condition, he again pleaded for death. God confronted him a second time. "Do you have a *right* to be angry about the vine?" God now confronted Jonah with what he could best understand—through his intellectual, moralistic, and legalistic mind. "I do," he replied, "I am angry enough to die."

What was the *right* about the vine he felt entitled to? Was it because it was the only thing left on earth that he felt some comfort from? Wasn't he justified to demand God's compassion for his suffering after what he felt he had done for the Lord? But God wanted Jonah to grasp the "big picture" to come closer to experience the warmth and compassion God had for Nineveh. Despite Jonah's assumption about who his Creator was, he was behaving as though the clay has the *right* to argue with the Potter on the eventual shape of things to come. God tenderly said to Jonah:

> You have been concerned about the vine, though you did not tend it or make it grow. It sprang up overnight and died overnight. But Nineveh has more than a hundred and thousand people (infants alone) who cannot tell their right hand from their left, and many cattle as well. Should I not be concerned about that great city? (Jonah 4:10)

At this, the Great Therapist had made the final interpretation. And it ended with a divine question.

Interpretation

We do not know what happened to Jonah and what his final response was or if he ever made one. God had the last word. The divine question prompts an answer not only from Jonah, but also from each one of us. God wanted Jonah to personally experience his divine will and compassion. Did Jonah get it?

The prophet Isaiah raised the question of the ultimate authority of God, "Does the clay say to the Potter, 'What are you making?'... Concerning things to come, do you question me about my children, or give me orders about the work of my hands? (Isaiah 45:9,11) The theological issue becomes the absolute sovereignty of God. Either God is supreme or God is not. That is the tautological question.

But God's will is intricately intertwined with the responses of man. The all-encompassing God redeems his people and wants to correct individual character flaws. For those called by God, he wants them to resonate with his nature and carry out his will.

A person's psychological make-up influences the cognitive, emotional and behavioral responses made to God's calling. It would appear far easier for God to create robots out of humans. But that was not his design. He provided man with choices. The beauty of it is that through God/human interaction, God's purposes are manifested and accomplished. Herein lies the relevance of attuning one's character to conform to God's own nature.

There were deeper psychological reasons for Jonah's refusal to preach to Nineveh. Was it because his audience was gentiles? Was he refusing to feel God's compassion? Or, was he incapable to feel at a deep emotional level? For whatever the reason, Jonah rationalized that it was God's fault, not his. He thought he knew better than God did. He must have reasoned that it was unjustified for God to put him through those horrifying experiences when it was within God's power to stop them. He held God responsible for causing the grief, shame, guilt and pain he felt. Jonah's self-centeredness and narcissism *was* his own idol, and he didn't realize that he was forfeiting grace by clinging to it.

His wounded narcissistic feelings sparked the anger that sprang from deep within his unconscious. According to Jonah there was his way or no way. He wasn't ready to look at himself or at his conscious or unconscious motives for running away from God's calling. God had to bring him to his senses, put him through extreme trials in order to make Jonah realize his flaws. And God was extremely patient with him. It was up to Jonah to answer the divine question.

Conclusion

The story of Jonah is usually used by evangelical Christian preachers to exhort Christians not to rebel against God's will but to faithfully carry out God's mission in their life. In this chapter, I focused on Jonah *the person*, his personality and to show how his rebellious character and self-centeredness hindered his ability to carry out God's will. Out of the interplay between Jonah's stubbornness, God's patience, and the circumstances in which the confrontation between Jonah and God took place, we can discern several spiritual messages:

1) God revealed his will in many ways, including the forces of nature, human responses, and the words spoken by his prophets. His divine purposes are achieved through men and women who stand ready to respond to his calling.
2) Inasmuch as God cares deeply about all people, God also is vitally interested in the edification of individuals he has called into his service. He requires that the character of his servants change and the transformation must include a fundamental change so that the character of the person called by God can resonate with God's nature and be able to do God's will. Having an intellectual understanding of God as Jonah had is not enough. The heart must align itself with what the mind professes to believe. And one must be willing to look within oneself in order to change.
3) Insight is difficult to achieve. There is a Chinese saying that it is easier to move mountain and river, but harder to change character. But character change is necessary for believers and particularly for God's servants. Often, as in individual psychotherapy, confrontation is necessary to achieve insight. Christ said, "Why do you look at the speck of sawdust in

your brother's eye and pay no attention to the plank in your own eye?" (Matthew 7:3) Divine confrontation, as in Jonah's case, may involve a greater scheme and may be difficult to understand and bear, particularly if it involves suffering. The "eyes of the heart" must discern the spiritual lessons and the meanings of suffering. Many times, our "idols" stand in the way of God's grace. They need to be removed so that the discerning mind and heart can hear the "gentle whisper of the Lord after the fire." (1 Kings 19:11) In Jonah's case, his self-centeredness or narcissism and his rebellious character stood in his way of God's grace. We have to listen to the psalmist who said:

> Search me, O God, and know my heart,
> Test me and know my anxious thoughts.
> See if there is any offensive way in me,
> And lead me in the way everlasting.
> (Psalms 139:23-24)

KEY POINTS:

- God was as interested in transforming Jonah as he was in saving the people of Nineveh.

- Repentance leads to salvation.

- Rebellion against God's will leads to calamity and suffering.

- God's will is revealed through the forces of nature, God/human interaction and his prophets.

- Jonah's self-centeredness and narcissism explain the paradox as to why he became enraged during his confrontation with God at the height of his success.

- The eyes of Jonah's heart were blind to the fact that God's compassion could triumph over his justice.

SECTION 3:

PATH TO SPIRITUALITY

8. Christ on Spirituality

SIGNIFICANCE:

Seek Spirituality. It is the secret to becoming empowered.

Christ

"I am the vine; you are the branches. If a man remains in me and I in him, he will bear much fruit...if you remain in me and my words remain in you, ask whatever you wish, and it will be given you." (John 15:5,7)

"... you will receive *power* when the Holy Spirit comes on you." (Acts 1:8)

I have discussed how Paul, Peter and James have emphasized the essential role of Christ in achieving Christian spirituality. Let us now see what Christ say about spirituality and how to achieve it. In John 15, Christ used the analogy of the vine and the branch to define this spiritual relationship. When a man *remains* in Christ and Christ's words are in him, that spiritual connection becomes the critical element in the re-establishment of the once-lost relationship with God (see Chapter 2). Acceptance of Christ's words and his teaching becomes the transforming power in achieving Christian spirituality. The belief in Christ invites the indwelling of the Holy Spirit. God's transforming words working through the Holy Spirit in the believers becomes the ingredient to Christian spirituality. And Christ, the Word incarnate, made it happen.

Christ said to his disciples, "God is spirit, and his worshipers must worship in spirit and in truth." (John 4:24) In other words, spirituality is a state of being and the way to understand it must be approached in an experiential way. Nicodemus, the Pharisee, educated and logical man that he was, like many of the contemporary scientific minds today, couldn't understand this phenomenon. When he approached Christ by night to inquire of his miracles, Christ told him to be "born again" in order to *see* the kingdom of God. (John 3:3) Nicodemus responded, "How can a man be born when he is old?" He didn't understand that Christ was using the metaphor to refer him to a new experience that can be seen only through *the eyes of the heart*. Christ elaborated to Nicodemus:

> I tell you the truth, no one can enter the kingdom of God unless he is born of water and the Spirit. Flesh gives birth to flesh, but the spirit gives birth to spirit...The wind blows whatever it pleases. You hear its sound, but you cannot tell where it comes from or where it is going. So it is with everyone born of the Spirit. (John 3:5-9)

Like wind that cannot be perceived by the physical eyes but its presence is felt through other senses, spiritual reality is seen and felt by the effects it produces. It is a human experience of a dimension of the third kind. The reality of the experience is validated through the "fruits" or the changed behavior in the life of the transformed person. That process of change is described by Christ as being born-again. It means the creation of a new spiritual being with a new state of mind that resonates with the nature of God (see Chapter two). This was the phenomenon that Nicodemus initially couldn't grasp. He did not understand that spiritual rebirth refers to the transformation of the mind, the heart and the total being of a person. And that transformational process begins with the acceptance of the words of Christ through faith. For the word of Christ to germinate and ultimately blossoms into a glorious life, a person has to accept the words of Christ through faith.

Thus, Christian spirituality cannot be separated from a relationship with Christ. And that relationship is maintained by keeping the words of Christ in one's mind and heart. Paul says it clearly, "For God was pleased to have his fullness dwell in him (Christ)." (Colossians 1:19) "To them (the saints), God has chosen to make known among the gentiles the glorious riches of this mystery, which is Christ in you, the hope of glory." (Colossians 1:27)

Christ in believers and believers in Christ, for both believing Jews and gentiles alike—that continual close and intimate contact with Christ—is the key to achieving and maintaining Christian spirituality. And the metaphor of the relationship between the vine and branches explicates this process. The spiritual state of a person without this special relationship is like being stuck on the physical world described in the book of Genesis: "the world was formless and empty, darkness was over the surface of the deep." The Spirit of God was "hovering over the waters" and has no effect on the individual. (Genesis 1:2) On the contrary, the Gospel of John describes the creation of the spiritual world when one is connected with God through Christ, "In the beginning was the Word, and the Word was with God, and the Word was God." (John 1:1) "Yet to all who received him, to those who believed in his name, he gave the right to become children of God—children born not of natural descent, nor of human decision or a husband's will, but born of God." (John 1:12-13) This is the rebirth that Christ taught Nicodemus. The Spirit of God that created the spiritual world is the Spirit that transforms mind. And in the new creation, the transforming of the mind is a spiritual act of re-birth, an act of the Spirit.

Earlier, we have seen through the writings of Paul, Peter and James (Chapters 2-4), how this transformational process works. First, there is acceptance of the words of Christ by faith. Then there is the in-dwelling of the Spirit. Finally, there is a process of daily continual death and renewal—death to the old 'self' and those depraved, self-centered traits; and alive to the new nature and characteristics of God. The new person now becomes empowered to rid him- or herself of things of the flesh, and "put on" the new man after the Spirit, whose nature conforms to God and the mind of Christ. And the transformation affects the totality of one's personality—in thinking, in feeling, in actions, in interpersonal relationships and in one's relation to the world. Since Christ also mentioned the critical role of the Holy Spirit in this process of spiritual empowerment, we shall now examine how this works.

The Role of the Holy Spirit

In Chapter two, Paul had already mentioned partly the role of the Holy Spirit in the lives of believer. This section briefly expands on a different aspect of the role of the Spirit—in the dispensing of spiritual gifts. But first, let me share my understanding of what the biblical Holy Spirit is.

In the Christian concept of a triune God, "three persons in one"—the Father, the Son and the Holy Spirit—each person seems to assume a different role at a different time. God the father was active during the creation of the world. God the son, Christ, was active during the redemptive phase when he came to die on the cross for the sins of the world. After Christ's death and resurrection, the Holy Spirit took over. Furthermore, the Holy Spirit clearly is intimately related to the life of Christ as mentioned in the bible:

- Christ is the result of the conception of the Holy Spirit with Mary. (Matthew 1:18)
- Jesus was baptized with the Holy Spirit. (Matthew 3:11, 16)
- Jesus was led by the Spirit into the desert to face his temptations. (Matthew 4:1)
- Jesus promises the coming of the Holy Spirit, the Spirit of truth. (John 14:16)

Jesus said, "It is for your good that I am going away. Unless I go away, the counselor will not come to you; but if I go, I will send him to you…when the spirit of truth comes, he will guide you to all truth. He will not speak on his own; he will speak only what he hears, and he will tell you what is yet to come. He will bring glory to me by taking from what is mine and making it known to you." (John 16:7-14)

Thus, the Spirit will assume a dynamic role in the life of believers. It will have a revelatory function to truth. The Spirit also empowers.

Paul prayed for the Ephesians to be strengthened with "power through his Spirit in your inner being. (Ephesians 3:16) The indwelling of the Spirit will guide and lead a man to a new level of understanding of Christ and God, a new spiritual revelation. Paul stated: "…that Christ may dwell in your hearts through faith. Being rooted and established in love, [you] may have power, together with all saints, to grasp how wide and long and high and deep is the love of Christ, and to know this love that surpasses knowledge—that you may be filled to the measure of the fullness of God." (Ephesians 3:17-19) Acquiring the "full measure of God" in Christ, this is the ultimate vision of the *eyes of the heart*. It is the attainment of a state of grace and spirituality when Christ takes over one's being, to be conformed to the nature of God and to be filled with knowledge of the fullness of God.

The Spirit also dispenses "gifts" or talents to be used for the edification of the church and for the common good. These gifts can be seen as instruments of empowerment. They are the means by which Christians can exercise their special talents. Paul speaks of nine gifts of the Spirit (I Corinthians 12:8-10). (Kluepfel defines the eight "gifts" of the Holy Spirit or "charisms"[1] which I summarize below. In addition, I have added the ninth "gift" that Paul mentioned for completeness sake.)

1. "The word of wisdom," "the ability to apply the facts and teachings of Christianity to the varied events and perplexities of the Christian life, the unction of devotional utterance."
2. "The word of knowledge" "the ability to present in due order and with clearness, the doctrines of Christianity, or its important facts in the confessions and by scientific theologians of the church."
3. "Faith." "Not the common faith in Christ, whereby one is justified before God, and obtains forgiveness of sins…but—a particular virtue or power of Spirit which He works in the church, so that some can do great and remarkable things with unwavering courage." (Luther)
4. "Gifts of healing," miraculous cure. "Is any sick among you? Let him call for the elders of the church and let them pray over him anointing him with oil in the name of the Lord." (James 5:14)
5. "Workings of miracles," operation of power. "All works of power besides those of healing: Peter's slaying Ananias and

Sapphira. (Acts 5:3) Paul's blinding Elymas the sorcerer (Acts 13:11); the raising of the dead. (Acts 9:40)"

6. "Prophesy," inspired utterance. "...the endowment which enabled a Christian to speak so as to bring the mind and spirit of the hearer into touch with God." (Expositor's Bible.) It functions for believers for their "strengthening, encouragement, and comfort." (1 Corinthians 14:3)

7. "Discerning of the Spirit." "The power to discern the real and internal qualifications of any person for an office, or to discover the inward workings of the mind by the Holy Spirit, as Peter did those of Ananias." (Acts 5:3) (Matthew Henry)

8. "Kinds of tongue," "...the common opinion of scholars is that gifts of tongue did not consist in ability to speak a foreign language even temporarily, but in an exalted frame of mind which found expression in sounds or words belonging to no human language...Probably all such manifestations are due to violent nervous agitation." (Expositor's Bible) Paul said the purpose of the "tongues" is a sign for unbelievers. (1 Corinthians 14:22)

9. "Interpreting of tongues,"[2] In 1 Corinthians 14, Paul explained the interpretation of tongue as the ability to interpret, in understandable languages, "tongues" spoken by others, so that the listener can know what is being spoken. It commands a higher order of utility for the listeners than speaking in "tongues" alone. (1 Corinthians 14:19)

These spiritual gifts are part of the "fruits" of the Holy Spirit Christ has spoken about and has promised the believers. In a way, they could be subsumed under the phenomenon of the "fruits" or behavioral manifestations that William James alluded to. They complement the role of the Spirit that Paul alluded to in Chapter two. The Spirit in believer becomes a dynamic force for change for the self and also to effect changes in the world. Thus, Christian spirituality is tied to a belief in Christ and in the dynamic role of the Holy Spirit working in the lives of the believers. The work of the Holy Spirit is responsible in the transformational process that is total and integrated. It elevates a person's spiritual dimension to new heights. It is empowering.

KEY POINTS:

- Christ teaches that the maintenance of an ongoing relationship with him by keeping his words and practicing his precepts is the secret of a vibrant Christian spiritual life.

- The Holy Spirit will guide believers to all truths, to discover and acquire their true talents, and to empower their lives.

- Christian spirituality cannot be separated from a belief in Christ and in the workings of the Holy Spirit.

Afterword

I have tried to illustrate within these pages how psychological insights can enhance scriptural understanding and vice versa from one faith tradition—through the Evangelical Christian perspective. I feel this is necessary not only because it would be a mammoth undertaking to discuss spirituality from the perspective of the world's major faith traditions, a task beyond what I was prepared to do, but also that by being too inclusive of all faith traditions, I could not do justice to an in-depth discussion of spirituality as it can be addressed in one faith tradition.

This book focuses on where the impact of a belief in the Christian God and Christ counts the most—on the transformation of the mind and of one's personality. Changing mindset and personality patterns are hard, as anyone who has gone through psychotherapy can attest to. Yet, to achieve a more fulfilling life sometimes we must change our self-defeating personality patterns as the lives of King Saul, King David and Jonah vividly demonstrate. Biblical exhortations and modern treatment approaches need not clash. Mental health professionals can offer therapeutic techniques to do so from the secular perspective. Biblical spiritual exhortations could provide the motivation and the inner strength to effect that change. They can complement each other to overcome gripping human helplessness and ailments. The *eyes of the heart* pointed us to the biblical path to achieve this inner strength to change. And I hope what I've tried to describe within these pages moves us a step closer to taking the necessary action to concern ourselves with the central core of our being—our spirituality—and to learn how to apply it to enrich our life.

Spiritual transformational power must be applied to and manifested in one's daily life if it is to be relevant. It is not enough to reduce faith to intellectualism. In reality, medical science has shown us the inseparability of thoughts, feeling, and memories.[1] The power of belief is shown by the fact that "believing and endorsing *cause* certain emotion to happen."[2] What we believe, how we feel and the values we have influence the way we conduct our lives. In this materialistic world, our culture is overrun with the superficiality of the transient. Wars, conflicts, man-made or nature-induced disasters are rampant. And debilitating anxiety, addictive habits, depression and despair are prevalent. Have our values in life been reduced to the attitude of the parable of the rich man: "Take life easy: eat, drink, and be merry?" (Luke 12:19, Isaiah 56:12) We find that a hunger and a need for spiritual revival are also apparent. Where and how can we find the spiritual power to fill this inner vacuum?

The New Testament tells us that two thousand years ago, the man of Galilee made his appearance on earth and expounded a way of life and for a change in the status quo for men and women to become the children of God—in thinking, feelings and actions. He taught us to look within ourselves first. He showed us the way to be in touch with the ultimate bliss of spirituality by entering into the "kingdom of God." He taught men and women the way of the spirit and the secret to a fruitful spiritual life. He challenged us to live for God and for others, to side with the truth, to be imbued with a mission of love and goodness, and to be the "light and salt" of this world. He reminded us that there must be a change in the heart and character for believers to become effective. ("If the salt loses its saltiness...it is no longer good for anything." [Matthew 5:13]) He urged us to live a life in order to give "light to everyone in the house...that they may see your good *deeds* and praise your Father in heaven." (Matthew 5:15-16) Above all, he promised the enlightenment and empowerment that can come by through the presence of the Holy Spirit in us when we put our faith into his words.

Christ's apostle, Paul, wanted us to know that the path to Christian spirituality must be experienced and discerned through *the eyes of heart*. The *eyes of the heart*s help us understand the transformational process that can empower our life and that also can give meaning to our existence. It suggests to us that the transformation process is total and involves all aspects of our personality – in thinking, feeling and actions— not just intellect alone. The inner empowerment of the spirit is actualized in the way we regard and care for our body, in our relation with others, in our relationship with the world, and in our relationship with God. Paul reminded the believers in Ephesus that despite the physical danger they faced, their struggle was not against flesh and blood, but against the rulers, against the authorities, against the powers of this dark world and against the spiritual forces of evil in the heavenly realms. (Ephesians 6:12) From Paul's perspective, one has to be ready at all times to fight the ever-present spiritual forces of evil in the world. Paul's admonition to the Ephesians is equally relevant today. In the fierce warfare between the forces of good and evil that we witness in our present world and that we encounter in our daily lives, Christian spirituality is a call to arms to be instruments of righteousness against the spiritual forces of evil. Believers are challenged to live for the common good.

So what is the final message of *the eyes of the heart*? Christ and his disciples all reminded us that if we truly seek spirituality, if we want to live life at a higher plane of happiness, if we want to be empowered and make a difference in the world, then we must listen to the transforming words of the man from Galilee — for Christ has shown us that he is the *way*, the *truth* and the *life*.

Endnotes

Preface

1. Abraham Herschel cautioned against taking these two extreme positions when interpreting the words of the prophets. I believe that caution is equally applicable here when using psychological concepts in interpreting biblical spirituality. Abraham Herschel, *The Prophets* (Peabody, Mass: The Prince Press, 2004), vii.

Chapter 1

1. Daniel E. Hall, Harold G. Koenig, Keith G. Meadow, "Conceptualizing 'religion': how language shapes and constrains knowledge in the study of religion and health" *Perspect Biol Med* 47 (2004): 386-401.
2. William James, *The Varieties of Religious Experience* (New Hyde Park, New York: University Books, 1963), 29. (original edition 1902)
3. Daniel E. Hall, Ann Marie Catanzaro, M. Ojinga Harrison, et al., "Religion, Spirituality, and Mysticism," *Am J Psychiatry* 161 (2004):1720-1721. (letter to the Editor)
4. Jordan Aumann, *Spiritual Theology* (Huntington, Indiana: Our Sunday Visitor, 1980), 17.
5. William James, *The Varieties of Religious Experience*, 29.

6. Wilkie Au, *By Way of the Heart: Toward a Holistic Christian Spirituality* (Mahwah, New Jersey: Paulist Press, 1989).

7. William James, *The Varieties of Religious Experience*, 31.

8. Ibid., 34.

9. Ibid.

10. Ibid.

11. Ibid., 35.

12. Ibid.

13. Ibid., 45.

14. Ibid., 46.

15. Barry L. Callen, *Authentic Spirituality: Moving beyond Mere Religion* (Grand Rapids, Michigan: Baker Academic, 2001), 17.

16. Arthur Kleinman and his colleagues at the Harvard School of Public Health introduced the concept of "sociosomatic" medicine, arguing for the integration of sociological and biological phenomena. The "mind in culture" is an extension of the sociosomatic concept. See Arthur Kleinman A, Anne E. Becker, "Sociosomatic": the contribution of anthropology to psychosomatic medicine. 60 (*Psychosom Med 1998*): 389-457.

17. Sir Edward Burnett Tylor, a British anthropologist, in 1871, provided this definition that is generally accepted as the first clear and comprehensive definition of culture. Edward Tylor, *Primitive Culture*, vol. 1 (Boston: Estes and Lauriat, 1874), 1.

18. Anthropologist Ward Goodenough described two orders of reality of culture: the subjective and objective. See Ward H. Goodenough, Comments on cultural revolution. 90 (*Daedalus,* 1961): 521-528.

19. Percepts, concepts, propositions, beliefs, values, and operating procedures (recipes) are considered components of culture. For a discussion of the components of culture, see Albert Gaw, *Concise Guide to Cross-Cultural Psychiatry* (Washington, DC: the American Psychiatric Publishing Inc, 2001), 10-14.

Chapter 2

1. I feel it's important to distinguish spiritual power from worldly political power and I am indebted to Jack Hill, M.D. for calling my attention to Gregory Boyd's writing about the two kinds of kingdom (of the world and of Jesus Christ) that distinguished how the two different types of power operate: "While all the versions of the kingdoms of the world acquire and exercise [power] *over* others, the kingdom of God, incarnated and modeled in the person of Jesus Christ advances by exercising power *under* others. It expands by manifesting the power of self-sacrificial, Calgary-like love." Gregory Boyd, *The Myth of a Christian Nation.* (Grand Rapids, Michigan: Zondervan, 2005), 14. See also Greek meanings of power in endnote 5.

2. Transcranial Magnetic Stimulation (TMS) is an experimental procedure that sends frequent burst of magnetic pulse through the scalp and skull into the brain, where it synchronizes with the electrical activity in the brain to treat various psychiatric conditions such as depression and insomnia.

3. The concept of sin is central to the Christian theology. As used in this volume, I am adopting Karl Menninger's definition of sin: "Sin is transgression of the law of God; disobedience of the divine will; moral failure. Sin is the failure to realize in conduct and character the moral ideal, at least as fully as possible under existing circumstances; failure to do as one ought towards one's fellow man (Webster)...Sin has a willful, defiant or disloyal quality; someone is defiled or offended or hurt. The willful disregard or sacrifice of the welfare of others for the welfare or the satisfaction of the self is an essential quality of the concept of sin." Karl Menninger, *Whatever Became of Sin?* (New York: Hawthorn Books, Inc, 1976), 18-19.

4. The bible frequently referred to the metaphor of blood. Blood is intimately linked to the sustenance of life and is basic to human viability and vitality. Leviticus 17:11 states, "For the life of the flesh is in the blood." The practice of

blood sacrifice gets very close to a theology of works in which by shedding the blood of animals we pay for the sins committed. This example indicates that we are saved by grace, not by our own works. Christ paid the price so that we can enjoy the new creative freedom. Dr. James Gordon Emerson, Jr. (Personal correspondence, April 26, 2007).

5. I thank Dr. James Gordon Emerson, Jr. for clarifying the Greek words for "power." *Dunamis* - from which we get the word "dynamite," is the ultimate power, something as large as the power of creation. The other word is *Energe* – from which we get the word energy, refers more to our work. Although there are earthly powers which we share such as the power of life and death in medical decision, above and beyond this, Christians can experience the power (the *dunamis*) of God that is qualitatively different from any earthly power (earthly *dunamis*). Thus the translation could have read: "...the immeasurable greatness of his *power* according to the workings of his great *energy*. God put this power to work in Christ when he raised him from the dead and seated him at his right hand in the heavenly places, far above all rule and authority and *power* and dominion..." Dr. James Gordon Emerson, Jr. (Personal Correspondence of April 26, 2007).

6. See Matthew Chapter 4:1-11.

7. Although emotion and feeling are intimately related, conceptually it is useful to note the distinction between the two. "Emotions are actions or movements, many of them public, visible to others as they occur in the face, in the voice, in specific behavior...Feelings, on the other hand, are always hidden, like all mental images are, unseen to anyone other than their rightful owner, the most private property of the organism in whose brain they occur." Antonio Damasio: *Looking for Spinoza - Joy, Sorrow and the Feeling Brain* (New York: Harcourt Press, 2003), 28.

Chapter 3

1. William Morris (Editor), *The American Heritage Dictionary of the English Language* (New York: The American Heritage Publishing Company, 1970), 1337, 1463.

Chapter 4

1. David P. Nystrom, *The NIV Commentary: James* (Grand Rapids, Michigan: Zondervan Publishing House, 1997).
2. Hershel Shanks, Ben Witherington III, *The Brothers of Jesus* (San Francisco: HarperCollins Publishers, 2003), 146.
3. Ibid., 146-151.
4. Ibid., 146.
5. Ibid.

Chapter 5

1. Judges were charismatic men (except Deborah) raised up by God who ruled the tribes of Israel during the era intervening from the death of Joshua (c. 1375 B.C.) to the era of Samuel (c. 1075). Unlike earthly king, they assumed a dual role: "delivering them from the powers of their enemies and administering the laws and rites of the Lord." Merrill F. Unger: *The New Unger's Bible Dictionary* (Chicago: Moody Press, 1988), 724-725.
2. *Self-esteem* is a psychological construct that refers to a person's feeling of being worthy and worthwhile. A person with sufficient self-esteem can accurately assess oneself and can value oneself successfully. This means being able "to realistically acknowledge one's strengths and limitations and at the same time accepting oneself as worthy and worthwhile without conditions or reservations." University of Texas at Austin, The Counseling and Mental Health Center. Better Self Esteem, 1999. http://www.utexas.edu/student/cmhc/booklets/selfesteem/selfes.html

3. For a description of these terms, please refer to the *Diagnostic and Statistical Manuel of Mental Disorders, Fourth Edition* (Washington, DC: American Psychiatric Association, 1994).

4. Freud postulated the presence of *unconscious mental mechanisms* to protect the individuals from painful ideas, feelings and drives. Some mechanisms such as humor and sublimation, (e.g. expression of aggression through games, sports or hobbies) are normal. Others such as psychotic denial, delusional projection, and distortion are pathological. In between these two extremes are other mechanisms such as rationalization ("a mechanism in which a person devises reassuring or self-serving, but incorrect, explanations for his or her own or others") (DSM-III-R), intellectualization, reaction formation and somatization. For a list and glossary of these terms, see George E. Vaillant: *Ego Mechanisms of Defense* (Washington, DC: American Psychiatric Press, 1992).

Chapter 6

1. BT Arnold, *1 and 2 Samuel: The NIV application commentary from biblical text—to contemporary life* (Grand Rapids, Mich: Zondervan, 2003).

2. Out of his lineage will come the Messiah.

Chapter 7

1. In psychology and psychiatry, *narcissism* refers to self-love. Some amount of this is healthy. However, excessive "infatuation and obsession with one's self to the exclusion of all others and the egotistic and ruthless pursuit of one's gratification, dominance and ambition" is excessive narcissism. (Sam Vaknim: Narcissism. MentalHelp.net. (http:/www. mentalhelp.net/poc/view_doc.php/type/doc/id/419).

Excessive narcissism becomes a narcissistic personality disorder when there is "a pervasive pattern of grandiosity, need for admiration, and lack of empathy that begins by early adulthood and is present in a variety of contexts." American Psychiatric Association: *Diagnostic and Statistical Manual of Mental Disorders, Fourth Edition.* (Washington, DC: American Psychiatric Association, 1994), 658-661.

Chapter 8

1. P. Kluepfel, *The Holy Spirit in the Life and Teachings of Jesus and the Early Christian Church* (Columbus, Ohio: The Lutheran Book Concern, 1929), 106-110.
2. Kluepfel mentioned the eight gifts of the Spirit. I added the ninth since this was mentioned in 1Corinthians and this gift has a specific "explanatory" function for those who speak in tongues.

Afterword

1. Antonio Damasio, *Looking for Spinoza - Joy, Sorrow, and the Feeling Brain* (New York: Harcourt, Inc., 2003).
2. Ibid., 93.

Index

Diagnostic and Statistical Manual 4th Edition of the, 174, 175
Amittai, prophet, 142
Ammonites, 103, 125
Amnon, 126
Amos, prophet, 142
Anger management, 53, 89
Antioch, 86
Aramaic language, 86
Armor of God
    putting on, 56
Araunah (the Jebusite),
    threshing floor of, 130, 133
        symbolism of the, 130, 133, 134
Ark of God. *See* God
Assyria, 142
Attitudinal change
    towards suffering. *See* suffering
Authentic life. *See* life

B
Bahurim, 128
Baptism, 41
Barrier separating man from God, 46
Bathsheba, 124-127
Be strong
    in the Lord, 59
Belief
    power of, xviii, 70
Believers
    "aliens" to the world, 67
    children of God, 40-41, 51
    co-heirs with Christ, 41
    co-workers with God, 47
    conscience of the, 50
    empowerment of the mind of, 40
    glorious new status of the, 67-72, 81
    God's workmanship, 47

D_____

I

Judah, 131
Judges, 104, 173
Judeo-Christian God, *See* Christian spirituality
Justification by faith in Christ, 86

K

Kidron Valley, 129
Kingdom
  of God
    born into, 158
    not of talk, but of power in, 47
  of heaven, 57, 87, 92, 94
Kiriath Jearim, 130
Knowledge of the great mystery of God,
  new, 43-46
Kluepfel P., 161, 175

L

Law
  of God, 39, 98, 171
  of sin, 39
Letting go of old habits, 40
Levites, 130
Life
  authentic, xv, xvii
    integration of faith and action in, 87
  forces
    direction of flow of, 45, 80, 81
  in Christ. *See* new life in Christ
  in blood, 71
  power. *See* power life
Light of the world. 37 *See also* salt
Live
  a good life, 72, 81
  a life
    of love as imitator of Christ's love, 53, 62
    worthy of one's calling, 52, 62

Q

Qualities
    God-like, 69

R

Rabbah, 125
Rahab, 95
Ramah, 119
Reconciliation through the cross, 46
Redemption
    through the blood of Christ, 42
    through the sacrifice of blood, 42
Relationship
    change in. *See also* slaves and masters; wives and husbands;
        children and parents; young people and elders; 55, 74
        church elders and parishioners, 74
Religion. *See also* spirituality
    abuse of, 25
    accepts the law of the universe wholeheartedly, 25
    art of winning the favors of the gods, 23
    "projections" of the unconscious mind in, xiii, 30
    contrast with spirituality in, 23
    definitions of, 23
    difference between casual and professional attitudes in, 24
    exceeding the moral frame of mind in, 25
    more personal branch of, 23, 25
    pure and faultless, 92
    total reaction upon life, 23, 24
    William James' definition of, 23, 24
Religious experience
    authenticity of, 24
Religious sentiment. *See also* religion
    authenticity of, 24
        actions as, 26
    harmful effect when applied in a distorted way, 25
    context of which positive or negative influence is exerted in, 25
Resisting temptation, 50

Righteousness
    breastplate of, 57
    God's people as instrument of, 56, 167
    of God through faith in Christ, 44
    persecuted because of, 87
Royal priesthood,
    Christ paving the way for believers to attain, 70
    offering of one's body as living sacrifice as a supreme act of, 70
    purification of "self" to attain, 70
    sanctification as a pre-requisite for, 70-71

S

Salvation
    helmet of, 58
    through faith in Christ, 68
Samaritan, 92
Samuel, prophet, 103, 104, 105, 106, 111
Sarah's womb, 44
Salt of the world. *See also* light
Saul
    anointed by prophet Samuel, 103
    background of his selection as the first king of Israel, 104
    battle with the Philistines, 104-105, 111
    character faults in, 104, 106, 107, 108, 109, 112-114, 115
    disobedience of, 105-106
    God's covenant and kingship of, 104, 115
    God's rejection of the kingship of, 105-106, 112
    emotional size of, 104, 107, 108, 113-114, 115
    emotional downward spiraling of, xviii, 110
    evil spirit from God visiting, 107, 108, 112
    interaction with David, 107-111, 122-124
    interaction with Jonathan, his son, 105, 109
    interplay of emotional state and spirituality in, 105, 106, 107, 111-114
    low self-esteem in, xvii, 104, 106, 108, 113-114
    mood swings of, 107, 112

T

somatization, 174
sublimation, 174
Unconscious mental life, xiv, 113, 174
Understanding God's will, 54, 129, 130, 135-137, 152
United Nations, 57
Unity of believers. *See* believers
Uriah, 88, 125
Uzzah, 130

V

Vaillant, George E., 174
Value(s)
    change of, 80
    of God, 68, 92, 94
    of the world, 39
Virtues. *See* spiritual virtues
Vine
    metaphor of connection with Christ, 48, 157

W

Waiting for the second coming of the Lord, 78
Wholesome thinking, xvii, 38
    definition, 66
Witch at Endor, 111
Wisdom
    asking God for, 91
    earthly, 91
    from heaven, 91-92
        characteristics of, 91, 98
        how to obtain, 91
    two kinds of, 91, 98
Wives. *See also* husbands
Word(s)
    becomes flesh, 47, 59
    of Christ, 66, 78
    of God,
        reflecting on the, 78-79, 90